Additional Testimonials for
Journey from Life to Life

"Where did we come from? Where are we going? Why are we here? In *Journey from Life to Life*, Dr. Krishna Bhatta uses a unique perspective to try understand the core and essence of our understanding of these three ultimate questions which all faiths try to explain. From his interactions with individuals who have faced death and life, and with much study of belief systems over several decades, Dr. Bhatta provides fresh ways of looking at ancient themes. We are given a comprehensive way of looking at who, what, and why we are. It is a read that is filled with the joys and challenges of life and obliges us to look into different possibilities in answering those eternal questions."

— The Reverend Colonel Andrew L. Gibson,
Joint Forces Headquarters Maine Chaplain

"In his new book, *Journey from Life to Life*, Krishna Bhatta, MD, provides a thorough and insightful review of Hindu spiritualism, offering clear explanations into meaning and purpose for this life and the pathway beyond."

— Jim VanKirk, MD, FACP,
Medical Director for Hospice & Palliative Care, Northern
Light Eastern Maine Medical Center, Bangor Maine

"*Journey from Life to Life* by Krishna Bhatta is an inspiring book for anyone interested in the ultimate journey of one's life. Individuals face a multitude of challenges and sometimes these challenges can be overwhelming and cause anxiety and fear. Most accounts of crisis in individuals and families focus on the symptoms and not the underlying causes. Spiritual and philosophical lessons can provide an anchor for people to understand the trials and tribulations in one's life journey. Bhatta is an experienced medical practitioner who realises the value of both spiritual and philosophical lessons in life and through his book *Journey from Life to Life,* he provides us with a useful tool."

—**Professor Biman C. Prasad,**
Leader of the Opposition National Federation Party
in Fiji, and Director, Fiji Institute of Applied Studies

"A beautifully written, compulsively readable, and extraordinarily sensitive explanation of the infrastructure that exists to support our lives and infrastructures that may exist at and after our deaths, this book outlines how to become successful in our life and how to start planning for the journey after death and the journey back to life. A must-read for anyone who wants to get to the truth regarding what life is all about."

—**Michael Levin,**
New York Times Bestselling Author

JOURNEY FROM
LIFE
TO
LIFE

Achieving Higher Purpose

KRISHNA BHATTA, MD

Redwood Publishing, LLC

Printed in the United States of America

First Printing, 2019

Published by Redwood Publishing, LLC (Ladera Ranch, California)
www.redwooddigitalpublishing.com

ISBN 978-1-947341-68-5 (paperback)
ISBN 978-1-947341-69-2 (e-book)

Library of Congress Cataloguing Number: 2019913139

Book Design:
  – Cover Design: Ana Mouriño
  – Interior Design: Ghislain Viau

10 9 8 7 6 5 4 3 2 1

JOURNEY FROM
LIFE
TO
LIFE

This book is dedicated to my mother and father.

"Experiencing the passing of my own mother, I can testify to the fact that Krishna's "take" on our journey is spot on! Very frank discussions revealed to me that my mother clearly saw her own life beyond her earthly life. And for those who have or know of others who have "seen the other side" during an out-of-body experience, I can confirm that although the journey may be difficult and painful, once one "lets go," the obstacles set before us disappear. *Journey from Life to Life* is the book for all those who are curious."

—**Elias Thomas,**
Project Leader, Rotary International

Author's Note

Dear Reader,

Before you dive into this book, it's imperative you read this note from me to you. I believe it will help to explain the reasons why I authored this book and why the information I've shared is so important.

The first thing I'd like to mention is that the chapters that follow require your undivided attention. Some of the topics are challenging and may need to be read more than once. However, I can promise you that you will finish this book feeling full of purpose and understanding about what comes next.

Having worked in the medical field since 1970, I have met all kinds of personalities from different continents and various sects and religions. This book is dedicated to every single one of those people.

My work, my workplace, and the patients of all ages whom I see day to day continue to inspire me. Have I met any unhappy patients or worked with discontented colleagues? Of course, I have! Who hasn't? But I've learned lessons from those encounters and moved on. Sometimes those individuals were in the wrong, while sometimes I was—but life carries on, and the net result is what truly matters.

Let me explain here the concept of *devta* and *devi,* as you'll be reading about these terms a lot throughout this book. In English, they translate to *god* and *goddess,* although that does not convey their *true* meaning. Without getting too in depth here, I will explain what devta and devi mean to me: it is that entity that inspires us or helps us in some way. Whether it's dev-*ta* or dev-*i* depends upon which gender we assign to them when recognizing them in our lives. For example, when I hit a golf shot in a tree, and the ball ends up on the fairway, it's the tree god assisting me, so it can be considered devta.

Those in the East took this concept to a different level, which they describe as, "achieving a higher purpose." I believe they are right to think that; we are all surrounded by natural forces of light, wind, water, and more.
- Can we be inspired by them?
- Can we draw energy from them?
- Can they support our growth in life?

This concept became the source of what in India we call the Ganges River: a devi, and the sun: a devta.

———— // ————

So how do devta and devi relate back to my patients? Let me tell you a story that was one of the things that motivated me to write this book. I once performed a surgery for bladder cancer on a nice, intelligent eighty-seven-year-old man in Bangor, Maine. After the surgery, he recovered reasonably well and went home. But after some time, he was hospitalized again for an unrelated infection, and the imaging studies found that his cancer had spread. His infection was treated, but he developed a *Clostridium difficile* infection, which can occur from the use of antibiotics and involves the intestinal tract. I used to visit him on my rounds each day, but one day stood out in particular. I still remember that he was in room number eight on the third floor. He was as nice, as conscientious, as polite, and as much of a "fighter" as he'd always been. He looked at me and asked me to sit down. As I took a seat beside him, I found him to be as peaceful as a Tibetan monk in meditation. He looked directly into my eyes and spoke these words:

"I want to go now."

I looked at him in amazement, and he appeared to be peacefully serious about what he was saying. I explained that we could treat his illness, but I refrained from pushing this treatment on him. He ended up dying a few days later. After that day, I couldn't help but ask myself the following questions:

Does he know where he is going?

Do I know where he is going?

These questions ignited my desire to write *Journey from Life to Life*, which I dedicate to all of my inspiring patients. I hope that this book will afford you a better idea of where you'd like to go and where you are going.

Yours sincerely,
Dr. Krishna Bhatta

Table of Contents

Acknowledgments

THIS BOOK WAS INSPIRED BY my patients. Without them, I may not have ever considered putting pen to paper and try to dissect the world of eastern thoughts; I dream of a world where eastern wisdom and western discoveries embrace each other and work together to achieve higher peaks. Words can't define my profound gratitude to each and every patient—past, present, and future.

A heartfelt thank you to Michael Levin for all his editorial assistance and making this project go from ideas in my head to a full and complete manuscript. Another big thank you to my copy editors and proofreaders who spent countless hours perfecting the copy. And last, but not least, thank you to Sara Stratton of Redwood Publishing for your dedication to the project.

Introduction

WHILE WRITING THIS BOOK, *Journey From Life to Life*, I found myself continually drawn to the village in which I grew up. No matter whom I talked to, whether they were literate or illiterate, whether they were rich or poor, whether they were from the upper caste or the lower caste, at one time or another, they engaged me in conversation related to their past life and/or their future life. If something good happened, they credited their good work in their past life or the good samskaras they carried on from that past life. As I grew into adulthood, I became curious about the meaning of this concept. The possibility of previous life and an afterlife touched the very core of my existence. I wanted to find out more, explore more. However, I eventually ended up outside India, where the concept of an afterlife was not in anyone's thoughts or conversation.

Every now and then, I was asked this question: "Do you believe in rebirth or reincarnation?" It used to irritate me, not so much because of the question itself, but because of what was being implied: "Do you *really* believe in reincarnation?"

Then I asked myself a question: "Why *shouldn't* they ask this question?" This concept is totally alien to them. They've had no discussions on this subject with their family members or friends.

There are several books written on the topic of life after death, including one by Deepak Chopra. Many of them speculate about what happens after death, but this book, the one I have written, discusses certain details of our present life that can help prepare us for the life beyond in our journey from life to life. I want my readers to know that this book does not address enlightenment or any other related topics in any detail simply because they are not part of the life-to-life journey. However, I do intend to address those issues in future books. Suffice it to say here that enlightenment is a journey that takes a person away from the cycle of births and rebirths; it marks the end of the journey from life to life. Now, the enlightened one can choose to be born if he so wishes to do.

I find that explanations about traditional Indian spiritual culture have often led to many misconceptions about certain teachings and tenets. For example, Westerners are generally introduced to meditation à la carte, removed from the context

of its native culture, where it is part of a holistic spiritual lifestyle. It's easy to understand what people seek to get from meditation; studies show it lowers blood pressure and can reduce the risk of heart disease. Proponents earnestly share how meditation has improved their mental clarity and focus.

All of that is good and has helped make the public aware of the benefits meditation can bring to our lives, but only in a secular context. It neglects to explain the true purpose of meditation. It's akin to taking a gummy vitamin; the sweet taste is a nice perk, but it's not the purpose of the pill.

The pioneers of meditation were not seeking a way to mitigate stress. They were not developing a methodology to elevate and stabilize mood levels in depression sufferers. I am not suggesting these things are unworthy goals; only that the forefathers of meditation, who lived some five thousand years ago, were aiming much higher. Rather than addressing any particular trouble in their daily lives, these men developed tools to help explore consciousness and beyond. They also developed meditation to assist them on the voyage from their present lives into their next lives, after death. Meditation was developed as a means of exploring the energy within, and to guide our paths and ease our burdens on the journey from life to life. This is its proper use and true power.

My intent is not to remove meditation from one box, where it is used for relieving blood pressure or treating diabetes, just to place it in another equally limiting container. Accomplished practitioners have developed many specific meditative practices for a variety of purposes, but in this book, we'll focus on meditation's greatest utility: expanding our awareness.

It's well known that the effects of exercise continue long after we stop working out. Similarly, when we expand our awareness beyond what is conscious, we continue to have a meditative mind throughout our day, our week, and even our lifetime. The things we learn, the way we look at the world and ourselves, and even our understanding of reality, stay with us, becoming an undercurrent. With this new awareness we can live more consciously and be more spiritually awake, and our thoughts and actions will begin to flow from this current.

Some of the ideas in this book will be thought-provoking and may require more than one read, but don't worry; I intend to address each of the main points brick by brick so that you'll finish this book feeling confident in your newfound knowledge. What you build upon this foundation of understanding could change your life—and your next life too. I will also slowly ease you into familiarity with the Sanskrit terminology we use to express these ideas. Sanskrit is an ancient language often referred to as the Latin of India, partly because of its distinct structural similarities to Latin, but also because Sanskrit was the language of the ancient scholarly elite, and it still carries that prestige today.

4

It's human nature to believe the things we have been taught to believe. My own life experiences and upbringing have prepared me for the ideas I speak about here. During my youth, my father would recite the verses of Gita, one of the world's great spiritual epics, as I listened in wonder. The love and reverence in my father's voice made a lasting impression upon me—as did the verses themselves—and I have never ceased studying those words. Although I spend more time in a robotic-surgery unit than in a temple or monastery, I have nevertheless devoted countless hours to studying and experiencing the underlying spiritual mysteries of life. In fact, I have spent as much time practicing meditation as I have practicing medicine. Yes, I am a surgeon, and not a *swami* or famous guru, but I do not believe that spirituality and spiritual exploration are only for those select individuals.

I offer the insights I have gained from experience, but also from life as a worker, husband, father, and grandfather, and they may differ at times from interpretations you have heard from other sources. So be it. The spiritual life is *for* us all and *of* us all, and there is space enough in the conversation for all of our voices. This is why for years I've presented lectures, writings, podcasts, songs, and video talks on Gita, Krishna, and other aspects of spirituality.

After spending time on three continents and studying apparent miracles of science and medicine, my interest in spiritual pursuits has deepened over time. One of my passions is for visiting temples and monasteries, meditating there, and meeting the rarest of the rare saints, *sadhus,* and *swamis* around the world. My love for the Himalayas takes me there often to experience the vastness, imbibe spirituality, and enjoy the thrill of traveling along some of the most dangerous roads in the world, such as the treacherous but beautiful highway between Leh and Manali. I am a man from the mainstream who has spent as much time with scientists as with saints.

Others will be led by their experiences and upbringing to wave certain aspects away as mere legend, and that's fine. Legends tend to start with something extraordinary, something truly remarkable that captures the imagination. This true thing then becomes the seed of the legend that grows from it through the years. The details often get muddied, but the heart generally remains.

Metallurgists in ancient India produced a remarkable type of steel called *wootz,* which was highly malleable when heated, but had extraordinary strength and toughness when cooled. Produced in South India and shipped to the Middle East, wootz was known as Damascus steel and was used to make swords for European crusaders, who reported that these "magical" swords were sharp enough to slice a feather floating in the air yet tough enough to use in battle. Over time the secret of making wootz was lost; even today we have not been able to replicate Damascus steel. All that was left behind were some archeological samples and an enduring legend, which is the type of situation that can occur when a chain of information is broken. However, it does not take anything away from the remarkable qualities of the steel that inspired the legend of magical swords.

Similarly, a plague, global nuclear war, or mass extinction could make modern digital technology unusable. After generations, the internet would only be known through stories told by older people. It would get harder for each new generation to believe such amazing devices that we currently take for granted ever existed, and eventually the internet could be seen as a myth.

The Sanskrit term for the succession of knowledge from one guru to the next is *parampara*. In India, our parampara, also called *guru-shishya*, is broken. Muslim raiders burned Buddhist libraries from Nalanda in the north. England colonized the nation, forcing the reeducation of an entire people. The chain was disrupted. Apparent miracles have slipped from our grasp because our parampara was broken. We now try to pick up the pieces, knowing in our hearts that we do far more than cling to antiquated cultural rituals; we are, in fact, reestablishing parampara—relearning what was forgotten.

For example, Indian children customarily touch their fathers' feet in greeting. Certainly this is a gesture of trust— some might say, submission—but the age-old custom stems from the practice of a father or guru transferring knowledge and spiritual energies through touch. This transfer, called *shaktipat,* is a deeply held part of eastern culture. I grew up with this system, touching the feet of elders whenever we met, in place of saying hello or shaking hands. It is hard to express to a person who is never exposed to this phenomenon the feelings and emotions that take place. When the prime minister of India, Shri Narendra Modi, touched the feet of an elder politician before filing his nomination in Varanasi, some called it the "photo of the year" for India.

While people today might find it difficult to believe this energy or well-wishes transfer is possible through this nonverbal communication, let me try to explain nonverbal communication via a story. I performed a major seven-to-eight–hour surgery on an eighty-one-year-old patient, who we'll call Joe. Surgery went very well. There was very little bleeding and patient's blood pressure remained normal throughout the procedure. However, Joe slipped into a coma after the surgery. The hospitalists, cardiologists, neurologists, and I performed all sorts of tests to figure out what might have caused him to go into a coma, and how to get him out of that state. We discovered no obvious cause for what occurred, and hence we did not know what to do to help him regain consciousness. His body was functioning fine and his recovery otherwise was unremarkable.

His wife, who we'll call Mary, was simply amazing, showing full confidence in the hospital and physicians. She never complained or showed any emotional upset. She had her own routine: She would sit down beside her husband every evening at around seven o'clock, hold his hand, and talk with him for about two hours, as if he were listening to every word she uttered. She would do that every night without fail, even though it was obviously a one-way conversation.

On the tenth or eleventh day post surgery, Mary noticed some finger movement. At first, she thought that she was imagining it, but then she felt Joe squeeze her hand. Tears streamed down her cheeks as she waved at the nurse with her other hand. It took a moment for the surprised nurse to figure out what was happening. Subsequently, Joe came out of his coma and was discharged within a few days.

I still don't know what kind of nonverbal communication took place between Mary and Joe, but in follow-up visits, Joe admitted to having had an out-of-body experience and claimed that he had been able to see—from a corner of the room—his own body lying on the bed and Mary holding his hand.

I often try to analyze how a nurse or doctor interacts with sick patients or the family members by their bedside in a hospital, but I never realized the value of nonverbal communication until recently, when I experienced it from the other side. I was a patient myself, and I was amazed to find out that a nice smile and a calming touch on the shoulder or hand meant so much more to me than the three-page consent form that described the procedure and its complications in great detail.

Nonverbal modes of communication are sometimes unexplainable. It might be hard to imagine that sometimes the act of saying nothing can give us the result we are looking for, but consider how commonplace things like radio waves and electricity are to us now, although they were unknown to previous cultures. What other natural forces might there be that we do not yet understand, but that we will someday be unable to imagine our lives without? It may be difficult to conceive of just what is meant by *spiritual energies,* but then again, I hear a lot of talk from top scientists about *dark matter* and *dark energy.* Maybe crediting the existence of something we can't detect by our usual methods isn't so outlandish after all.

While ancient Indian civilization boasted many technological achievements in addition to wootz, it is not what they were all about. The chief focus of Hindus for thousands of years was not on the external world, but on the *internal* world. The chief driving force of that civilization came from within and was directed within. Who can say, then, what wonders thousands of years of inward effort and research into consciousness—and beyond—might yield. Why not something so simple as the transmission of understanding via a gentle touch from a wise person?

Many people might recoil from such thoughts. Perhaps it's only because they currently lack the foundation of knowledge to prepare them for the information. Or perhaps they have simply closed their minds to new ideas. Such rigidness is the death of learning. However, one person cannot lead another to wisdom; we must find it for ourselves.

For millennia before we became aware of them, microorganisms were all around us, affecting our lives. Our ignorance gave us no protection from them, but our understanding does.

The pull of the moon's gravity affects the tides whether or not we understand how this occurs. Denying the existence of this gravitational pull will not calm the oceans.

This journey is our journey. It is happening whether we are aware of it or not, whether we believe or not.

Using this book as a platform, I hope to share Indian culture and its ancient truths so that you too may experience them. You can be a part of these practices and traditions, and you can feel deep connections with this ancient wisdom and with a great community of spiritual seekers who look within themselves for the betterment of all.

I invite you to embrace these truths and to make a practice of meditation. It can help you release the baggage you have acquired in this life and in previous lives. It can help you navigate your journey through this life and help you consciously transition into your next life. Far from being a life hack or a five-minute fix, meditation is the key to developing a powerful spiritual undercurrent in your life. And when we improve ourselves, we improve our world.

CHAPTER 1

Our Universe: A Structured Chaos —The Infrastructure

A T FIRST GLANCE, OUR UNIVERSE seems chaotic. But if we look closer, we see that even chaos is structured. Vast galaxies with trillions of stars follow predictable patterns, guided by the same rules as though gliding along parallel tracks. Ancient Indians learned that everything we know—and do not yet know—is laid out in a way that modern people would call *fractal*. However large a lens we use, or however much we narrow our scope, we see the same structures, the same forces, and the same patterns repeating.

In the solar system we call home, which contains a sun and a handful of planets orbiting the sun—the object of greatest mass—is a tiny part of the familiar spiral galaxy we call the Milky Way. It is just one element on the arm of another, larger

JOURNEY FROM LIFE TO LIFE

spiral gyrating around an enormously powerful center of gravity that is far, far away. Our galaxy, the Milky Way, and its larger siblings are all moved and guided by the same forces.

This beautiful blue planet we live on follows the same rules and runs on the same tracks as everything else in the universe. The particular conditions on our planet have made it inhabitable by life as we know it. Earth is warmed by the sun, which provides a constant stream of new energy to the system. This powers the hydrologic system, the water cycle of rainfall, condensation, evaporation, and rainfall again. The systems of sun and rain feed the plant life that, in turn, feeds animal life, until it is time for them to fertilize the plants, and so it continues.

Systems within systems exist here on our planet, and have done so for an almost unthinkable amount of time. And it doesn't much matter how it all started. Humans have developed many theories about how Earth came to exist, but more important than that intellectual enterprise is the certainty that it *does* exist. It is here, it works, and it does so in certain knowable ways. Regardless of one's beliefs, we know it to be so. I find this to be the most truly interesting and useful part of the cosmological discussion.

When we are curious about how things work, we begin to learn things of value. Then we begin to set up infrastructures. We set social structures in place, beginning with the cellular family and expanding outward to extended families, townships, nations, and unions of nations.

To support these social systems, we set up infrastructure systems, such as a water supply, sewage-treatment plants, electrical grids, telecommunication arrays, all the way to nationally owned and maintained satellite networks. We set up systems for governance, for civic and personal defense, for education, and so on, all to help our lives run smoothly.

There exists from the earliest times another infrastructure. Within that system, souls travel from birth into life, enter an unseen world through death, and come back to be born into the more familiar world again. This spiritual infrastructure is less often recognized than many others. Many who glimpse it think they alone have discovered some vast secret and seek to monopolize it. They will claim that *only they* have access to it, and seek to set themselves up as the gatekeepers to the unseen realm of the spirit.

Others come to learn that any number of people throughout the ages have made similar or related discoveries of the gates and bridges leading to that vast land. Many think that perhaps one passage to the unseen realm is the same as any other. Some doubt that a world beyond our world exists at all, and dismiss the discoveries as merely fantastical or wishful thinking.

As author Arthur C. Clarke famously pointed out, "Any sufficiently advanced technology is indistinguishable from magic." As such, many of the mechanics involved in the soul's journey from life to life certainly seem magical, mysterious, and perhaps even unlikely. But consider this: until Newton explained gravitational pull, it must have seemed like a strange, unknowable thing. An object that was on the shelf one moment and on the ground the next was thought to have been moved by a mysterious hand simply because people didn't yet understand how gravity works.

Although it was simple enough to see that gravity exists, people didn't truly understand *why it works.* Newton needed to explain that Earth's enormous mass exerts a force (gravity) that attracts other objects. That force existed every day for millions of years before the birth of Newton and his subsequent discoveries of the laws of physics, but until he explained it, gravity was unknowable and mysterious—and even then, many thought it unlikely.

In time, Einstein furthered our understanding of this natural force by showing that all objects with mass have their own gravity. The larger an object's mass, the stronger the gravitational pull it exerts, and since Earth is the most massive thing near us, it is clear why we are more drawn to it than we are to anything on its surface.

I'm using gravity simply to serve as an example of how an unseen framework—in this case, an element of physics—controls events whether we know about it or not.

Our world is filled with numerous frameworks and many infrastructures that have been there all along, regardless of our awareness. Certain Christian sects teach that the act of churning butter—which they still do by hand—is a form of prayer, and it is only by the direct intervention of God that butter is formed from the milk. You and I have other explanations for this transformation—that mechanical agitation causes the individual globules of the milk's fat to clump together, forming larger masses of milk fat that separate from the remaining liquid and become butter.

This process of butter making can be further understood by studying the microscopic nature of the fat globules. If one is familiar with the world on that scale, one will learn that the mechanical agitation breaks the fragile membranes of individual fat cells, and this is what allows them to clump together, forming greater masses of milk fat, or butter. So here we have a familiar everyday thing we can all readily understand based on our knowledge of certain frameworks and systems. But to some who lack an understanding of the frameworks involved, making butter is a miracle directly from the hands of God—an unknowable process.

In essence, the concepts in this book are no different. Although they may seem exotic or unlikely, they follow a framework of their own, governed by certain rules. Hindus have discovered many of these rules and workings through centuries of experimentation and observation. Some things remain unknown to us, just as much about physics continues to mystify scientists after three hundred years of constant efforts to unravel its secrets. What we do know is enormously enriching, and continued exploration will surely lead to deeper understandings.

Before we could enjoy many of the things we take for granted today, we needed to explore systems and frameworks that existed in the world from the start. Sunlight warmed our world from the beginning, and even with just a rudimentary understanding of its power, we were able to use the sun to our advantage. But until we had some understanding of thermodynamics and the movements of ions, we couldn't make solar panels to harness that energy and convert it to electricity. That's why it's beneficial to explore what we know about the nature of our life's journey and the spiritual infrastructure of our world.

The skeptical may doubt the value of such an exploration, a common response when seeking the unknown. The space race between the United States and the Soviet Union, which eventually led to sending a human to the moon, was financially expensive. Many Americans criticized the enormous amount of money spent. But half a century later we can clearly see that the technology developed for that endeavor paved the way for microcomputers, cell phones, the internet, and countless other advances that benefitted mankind.

One thing we may expect to gain from exploration of the spiritual infrastructure is a better ability to plan the trajectory of our lives. We know a great deal about our journey from life to death, and have a good understanding of many systems affecting that part of our existence. We have worked for centuries to set up infrastructures—economic, agricultural, administrative, etc.—to help us navigate the span of a single life. But Hindus discovered eons ago that we live not one life, but multiple lives, and these lives are each simply individual legs of one great journey.

Hindus are not alone in this knowledge of a life beyond life. Many cultures across the globe have some understanding and have caught a glimpse of a life beyond the one we now know, beyond the flesh we now inhabit. Still, the vast majority of us plan for only the particulars of this single lifetime, but leave what happens after death up to faith. Some hold to a tradition of an afterlife in which they will live on after the death of their earthly body. Others expect to be reborn in another physical form here on Earth. Most leave the details up to God and consider the matter settled.

I find that behavior peculiar. We rush to make a plan for the minutiae of this life, but even those who expect another *entire life* beyond this one do little to plan for it. When going on vacation, we do not fail to make reservations. We do not neglect to fill the gas tank when taking a road trip. We do not arrive at the airport and purchase tickets for the next airplane leaving that day, and leave it to fate where exactly we will spend our holiday—a prospect most people would find distressing.

We plan these trips. We often obsess over these getaways, and try to pack as much enjoyment, adventure, and activity into each day as possible.

The same can be said for many other aspects of our lives. We seek to eliminate waste from our workday. We try to optimize our educational experiences. We sweat and toil to make a family get-together pleasant and memorable. But an entire lifetime after this one, we leave to God.

I suspect that this is largely the case because we lack an understanding of the infrastructure of our spiritual journey. In other times, Indians spent thousands of years seeking to understand the infrastructure of our journey from life to life. Today, people all over the world have shifted their attention away from the spirit and toward the material. I do not condemn this; we have learned a great deal about our world and the underlying structures that guide its movement. Numerous advancements have tripled life spans, increased general prosperity, and reduced suffering. I am grateful for those advances. I am simply suggesting that if we were to apply the same energy on understanding the spiritual that we have on understanding the physical, we may see similarly spectacular results there as well.

We owe it to ourselves to dig deeper into the spiritual infrastructure with all the means and methods we now have at our disposal. We owe it to this and future generations to learn more about this field of study and put what we know to work. Just as learning germ theory led to vaccines, and learning about DNA gave us the ability to head off crippling genetic disorders, gaining a deeper understanding of the underlying principles of our spiritual journey can improve life for all humankind.

Think of the differences between the life of someone born into a wealthy family and a person born into poverty. People talk about the privilege of birth, but they know nothing of how we might shape that birth. Aside from financial well-being, which yields obvious benefits, there are other considerations that might be addressed by careful future-life planning. Buddha said he would come back to Earth one day, but it takes a special set of circumstances to bring about such an exceptional individual.

In my present lifetime there have been efforts by theosophists to set up such conditions. Jiddu Krishnamurti was groomed to be a vessel for Buddha's return; he was meant to surrender his own physical body so that Buddha could step in and walk among us again. This was unsuccessful; Krishnamurti chose to remain in his own body and teach in Buddha's stead, but at the very least, it was an interesting experiment.

While Krishnamurti himself had a distinguished career as an explorer and educator in the spiritual field, who can say what further and concerted experimentation might yield? Some say that there are always one hundred enlightened persons in the holy city of Varanasi. I cannot say if that's true, but

21

it could certainly be possible someday to have one hundred enlightened persons working together like a NASA-designed project to explore the spirit rather than space.

For too long, seekers of the spiritual infrastructure have been somewhat solitary explorers, hunting on their own for answers that can benefit us all. In my own time at medical school, a few of my fellow students and I would practice meditation, and we were regarded with unease. From its earliest days, the United States has been accepting of religions and belief systems. But while spiritual seekers of various stripes are tolerated, often underlying that tolerance is mistrust or confusion.

In my experience, there's not a social infrastructure to promote seekers or aid them in their journey. Instead, the focus is on seeing them become unimpeded in their actions. This is something upon which our generations should improve. A cultural attitude of tolerance provides a field we can sow to grow a new structure. Then together rather than separately, and scientifically rather than subjectively, we can begin to support and encourage exploration of the spiritual infrastructure that governs the journey from life to life. I dare to hope such a joint effort would produce results as effective and widespread as those infrastructures we have created that serve us in a single lifetime.

Self-sustainment is one system that shapes and enables our great journey. This is not to say that God is not present or uninvolved. The hand of the Divine set the system in place, but now that things are in operation, they run with a measure of independence. Likewise, the daily operation of our world does not require our direct intervention to make ordinary processes continue, although making corrections to keep the infrastructure of life running smoothly is our responsibility. By that, I mean the living are responsible and empowered to be its stewards. We can and should take care that our actions don't foul up the works and make it difficult for others to prosper on their own life journey. We also can and should improve our world and its institutions when we have the opportunity. The power and the responsibility are in our hands.

While a great visionary may arise now and again to make a significant improvement to our world, it occurs only rarely. And those great ones depend on the help of others who share their vision and help carry the burden of change, which requires work, as does the simple maintenance of the systems that enable us to continue our journey in a productive way. There are no idle passengers on this journey from life to life; everyone must play an active part in the process.

Much of what was known by the ancient Hindus has been lost to us, so we must work to regain it. We should consider it our personal task rather than a job for some luminary. We need not wait for the next Jesus Christ or the next Buddha. Neither of those men waited for someone else to take the wheel. Stephen Hawking did not become great by waiting for the next Isaac Newton.

Since we are all on this journey from life to life, it benefits us to gain a deeper understanding of the guiding factors that influence our paths. It's common to think that you are under-qualified to receive this knowledge, or that your connection to the Divine is largely unexplored territory, but that is true for most of us! You have more potential than you know, and that potential has brought you to this line of inquiry and to this book.

Babies are not born into a vacuum, but into a family. Likewise, we are born into a community, township, county, state, and nation, each influencing the path of our new life. Within all of these frameworks are other governing structures. Within a family, there may be a hierarchy of sons and daughters arranged by age, each having certain privileges and responsibilities. Within a community, there are social classes to which one belongs. Again, there exist certain responsibilities and privileges allotted to various classes, and we see varying levels of access to education, occupational opportunities, and the like.

Looking at the frameworks that already exist when a new life enters the world, we can begin to see the directions this life may take. *Should I go to trade school or work my way up to become a supervisor in the mine? Should I practice law or medicine? Should I marry and start a family or become a monk?* We all have different options available to us, and not all options will remain available at different times in our lives. This is readily understood, as different lives will present different opportunities—and some doors, once closed, never reopen.

Think of someone taking public office. They don't step into a void and try to figure out the job all on their own, without any guidance or support. The office existed prior to their entrance and will continue after their exit because there is an infrastructure in place. There are advisors. There are powers and capabilities attached to the office, and a staff waiting to carry out the orders of the person who holds it. There are also checks and balances to keep the power of the office from making people's lives terrible instead of enriching them. There exists a system to pay the people involved in the running of the office and a network of communications to help everyone stay connected and on task.

We may also see that there is an end or limit to these powers and privileges. A man who serves as governor of a wealthy and influential state will not have access to these abilities and perks once he steps down from that office. All things of this world are temporary, and some are more temporary than others. So it is as we move along the path of our journey.

The infrastructure of life as we know it is governed by certain principles; perhaps chief among them is karma. We will discuss karma at length in later chapters, but for now, I just want to point out its similarity to Newton's third law of motion, which states that for every action there is an equal and opposite reaction. In our daily lives, actions have powerful consequences. Just as we see ripples spread across a pond when we throw a pebble into it, so too can our actions cause disturbances. We may not be able to see the ripples we cause, but wherever we have effected a change, there will be consequences. This is especially true of actions that have a negative impact on another's life journey.

Not all actions cause disruption, however. Some actions are simply natural movement, the way fish beneath the surface of a pond never disturb the water on top. These actions carry no burden. One is not "good," and the other, "bad"; they are simply different.

If we call this life a journey, it's a small thing to imagine that there must be a pathway to follow, with various forks and branches that will take us in different directions. Expand this in your imagination to a network of highways spanning the entirety of the world we know. Smaller streets and alleyways connect to the greater highways like capillaries and veins to arteries, providing access to the entire world. We may imagine this to be a metaphor for the infrastructure that shapes and enables our journey from life to life.

We must now add vast, shining bridges leading to an unseen world beyond this one. Great people have—with the aid of many who worked side by side with them or labored for centuries after the passing of their leaders—constructed various bridges to allow us greater access to this other world. Before their works were in place, there was only the one known pathway to this world, and that was through death. Now that these bridges are built, accomplished seekers can use them to gain limited access to that land beyond the world we know.

Many of us don't know the unseen land because it is beyond our experience in this lifetime, and this is the only life we understand. This makes skeptics of some, while others cultivate a belief in its presence. Hindus do not *believe* in the other world any more than we *believe* in black holes, which are also invisible to us. We know of them due to work performed by the greatest minds of many centuries. While we cannot detect the other world with our ordinary consciousness, we have learned from our teachers' firsthand experience, and we understand that we may put in the work to touch it ourselves.

This may sound too good to be true, but consider a few things we now know that seemed incredible earlier in human history. The speed of light is 186,282.4 miles per second, but before we developed the technology to measure it, that would have seemed a preposterous claim. Now we know and accept the truth of it. The visible light we see is only a portion of wavelengths that exist. These higher and lower wavelengths of radiation are now known to us and have been harnessed by our technologies to do things that would have seemed impossible—or magical—to our ancestors.

We know that we can hear only a limited range of frequencies. But we use ultrasound to see through living tissue. We know that microscopic organisms too small to see—and not evil spirits—cause disease. We measure and map the surface temperature of the sun. All of this is possible thanks to the work of pioneers, thinkers, and risk-takers exploring the infrastructure of the physical world and paving the way for ever-greater discovery and utility.

The pioneers of the space race had to overcome many hurdles. Teams of scientists and engineers had to build frameworks that would allow them to pursue space exploration. Like Newton, they had to invent their own disciplines to describe the challenges they faced and develop new specialties within science to overcome those challenges. And though the cost was high and the work was dangerous, forces aligned to make their efforts successful.

This is another aspect of the spiritual infrastructure: there are unseen forces working to hinder or to help us in our endeavors. If we do ill, there are energies out there in the universe that seek us out and work to further our goals. People refer to them as "evil spirits" and many other names, but whatever we call them, they come when summoned. There are also forces—call them "angels," "good spirits," or whatever you'd like—that will align with us and complement our efforts when we do something noble. When we seek to lift others up instead of tread on them, when we work to elevate rather than belittle, these forces lend their energies to aid us.

Some will attribute the results of these assistive energies to luck, but Hindus have learned that the sympathetic vibration of like energies attracting like can be counted upon. Nothing guarantees success in any endeavor, but you may be surprised how much a previously unknown path reveals itself if you have the courage to walk in the fog a little while. It may be revealed that the unseen infrastructure was at your feet the entire time, just as physical infrastructures governing our world were there long before anyone discovered them.

When Buddha left the palace of his early years, he didn't know what he'd find. He would go from one teacher to another, learning what he could, and then moving on to another stretch of road that revealed itself when he was ready for it. His path was seldom clear to him and rarely easy, but life isn't meant to be easy. Growth only occurs when we push past what's familiar. Progress comes out of such discomfort, and we learn incrementally; we're shown what we're ready to see in that given moment. In time, Buddha's journey led him to enlightenment, and he saw the unseen world with clear eyes. Then he worked to build a bridge to it so that we could all profit from his journey.

Since time immemorial, seekers have built bridges, access points, and waymarks to the world beyond the one we sense with our physical bodies. These bridges were built by Guru Nanak (founder of the Sikh religion), Buddha, and others, but must now be maintained by those of us who wish to benefit from them. The entire network of roads and pathways laid down by the Divine to facilitate our journey of self-discovery must be maintained as well, and it falls upon those using them to do the work.

This does not contradict my earlier statement about the self-maintaining nature of our world because the system is self-regulating in a similar way to a richly diverse ecosystem such as a fish tank, which requires very little care. Responding to light and some nutrients in the water, algae grow on the rocks and glass. Plants compete with the algae to keep populations in check and improve the water quality. Tiny snails eat the algae, cleaning the tank. Guppies eat the snails and perhaps nibble at the plants. The plants use the fish droppings as fertilizer. Decomposing plant and animal matter pumps nutrients back into the system, which feeds the various types of plants and algae, which, in turn, feed the smaller creatures, and the cycle continues.

Every so often you need to add a little water or change a light bulb, but otherwise, the system takes care of itself. Such a system works because every form of life has a job within the infrastructure that the human caretaker has provided. If everything does its job, things move along with a good deal of sustainability.

This example is like a microcosm of life in our world, in the infrastructure laid down by the Divine. We all have different jobs, but they all feed into maintaining the infrastructure, or the ecological balance, if you like. To that end, each of us must avoid doing damage to the system or obstructing the life journey of another.

A parent provides entry, support, and early instruction to souls in the early years of their life journey. Those working in a variety of governing bodies keep societies functioning and prevent lawlessness. The flow of our journey should be free from obstructions; some of us—such as police and soldiers—do the work of clearing these obstructions. Those who devote themselves to spiritual practice seek new routes to lay paths to divinity or advise others in navigating what paths are available.

In this infrastructure, we each do our jobs and move forward in our journey from life to life. Very little direct intervention is required from the Divine to keep the system running smoothly. The power over our lives is in our hands. That is one of the points I most hope you take away from this book. We are in control, and we must do the work to make our lives what we wish them to be. One way to do this is by using our hard-won understanding of the spiritual infrastructure and the discoveries of seekers through the ages to help us plan our lives, meaning this life and the ones beyond.

Knowledge of infrastructure is powerful. Learning about infrastructures should not be merely theoretical. It has to be practical, and it should have applications in our lives. The following are some valuable questions for us to consider as we continue our journey from life to life.

- Do we understand, acknowledge, and appreciate that we are all born in an existing infrastructure?

- How do we sustain, maintain, and nourish existing good infrastructures?

- How do we protect these infrastructures from being destroyed? (The invaders burned great libraries in India and destroyed the existing education system there.)

- How can we be innovative and build new infrastructures for a better world?

- Does our social structure support the development and growth of a spiritual infrastructure?

The answers to these questions help us understand the importance of the support structure that exists around us; we all can and should contribute to make the infrastructure a little better than it was when we arrived.

Next we'll explore the five pillars, especially the one most important in terms of self-determination: the platform.

CHAPTER 2

The Five Pillars of Success—
The Platform

A S WE MOVE THROUGH THE world doing the work necessary to sustain our lives and to fulfill our unique individual purposes, we will come across obstacles and factors that limit our success. The greater the goal, the greater the difficulties. It's easier to feed oneself than it is to feed a family; feeding some friends at a dinner party will be simpler than feeding a starving mass of refugees forced to flee their homeland.

Serious-minded people who wish to accomplish things in our world might seek out secrets of success—from individuals, from books, from many other sources—to help them accomplish their goals. However, centuries ago, Bhagavad Gita laid out the five pillars, a universal formula for success.

Hey, Arjun the great.

There are just five pillars that

Are described by the Sankhya Philosophy

For accomplishments in all

Fields of any and all work.

The platform (Adhishthanam) is the first and foremost.

The Individual (Karta) or Individuals is the second.

Means, Tools, or call it Technology (Karanam) is the third.

Various kinds of all possible Efforts (Prithak Vidham),
    the fourth, and

The Unseen One, call it the Divine (Daivam) or

Call it Luck, is the final and the fifth.

— Bhagavad Gita 18:13–14

This verse from the final chapter of Gita illustrates the five key aspects that influence any endeavor. The platform represents a person's position of authority. This could be the head of household, a business owner, a member of parliament, a dictator, and so on. Different platforms afford a person varying levels of power and capability to impose his or her way of thinking on our world.

The second pillar—the individual(s)—refers to the specific qualities of those attempting an undertaking. Donald Trump and his predecessor, Barack Obama, both occupied the office of president, but each behaved very differently and achieved different results. What makes them different is that they are very different people, and that is the crux of this pillar. Two

34

individuals, even identical twins, will emerge at any given moment from the journeys of their lives as distinctly different people. The experiences, opportunities, and challenges they have known along the path forge them into differently capable individuals, and this has an enormous impact on the results of their efforts.

We describe the third pillar as a tool, or the available technology an individual has access to when attempting to produce an intended result. Robotic-surgery methods enable surgeons to produce results that are different from those produced when performing the same surgery with a scalpel and a flashlight. A soldier with an automatic weapon will have better odds of victory than if he were using a leather slingshot to propel rocks at the enemy. A student with internet access will be better able to research subjects than he would with an outdated encyclopedia. The right tools can make all the difference in any type of work.

The pillar of efforts describes various strategies we might employ to achieve a goal. For example, if a foreign country is causing a humanitarian crisis and appeals to its leader fail, perhaps trade embargoes or a covert campaign to undermine the leader's power and popular support might succeed. We could also try strategic military strikes or an all-out invasion. The more options there are, the greater the chances of success in any effort.

The final pillar is the Divine. Those with worldviews different from mine may call it "luck," but I understand it another way. Rather than random chance, this element of success is seen as the right person taking the right actions for the right reasons. When this occurs, seemingly random occurrences take place to aid someone in his or her purpose. It is out of our hands, of course, but the more we strive to do right, the more likely we are to receive the benefit of this phenomenon.

Of all the pillars, this platform is most important because it allows a person to gain the authority of position to make things happen as he or she thinks they should in whatever position that individual holds.

I recall Mahatma Gandhi once saying that good people should not enter politics. Given his stance in the 1930s that the state was a soulless machine that "represents violence in a concentrated and organized form," I can see why he said this. Still, I cannot help but think that the world is better because he ignored his own advice. Good people are precisely who we need in governance and in all positions of power and authority. If the state is a machine of organized violence, then who is a better candidate to stand at the controls than a self-described "soldier of peace" such as Gandhi?

Most platforms have much less power at hand than the leader of a country. But those who occupy those positions still have certain powers and responsibilities. Each day they make decisions based on their conscience and intellect that affect the people around them. We want good people in these positions, however great or small, rather than the good people deciding that only someone who enjoys power should seek it.

When I took on the rather modest mantles of chief of urology and director of urologic surgery at my hospital, my wife asked, "Why would you want that headache?"

My answer to her came from the Greek philosopher Plato, who once warned that if we do not each fulfill the highest function we are capable of, it's likely that an inferior candidate will take on the role. Failure to step up and participate fully often leads to being dictated to by someone who makes worse decisions than you would have made.

How often have you noticed in your professional life that the one making the decisions seems to know less about what's going on than anyone else? With all due respect to my wonderful colleagues, it seemed better that I take on the headache than risk these platforms being occupied by someone less appreciative of the responsibilities they entail or by someone who would make choices that I disapprove of.

Imagine if George Washington had chosen to sit at home after the American Revolution and enjoy his leisure instead of serving eight years as the first US president. How differently might the fledgling nation have fared? Washington's careful hand shaped much of the nation's character and future. If all good people choose to let someone else make the decisions, who then will be in charge but the less-than-good people?

We cannot demur and leave platforms of power in the hands of those who simply wish to throw their weight around and seek more power.

Sometimes that means we must behave in ways we'd rather not. I spoke to political strategists during India's last elections, and they were very open with me. They told me that to obtain a position that enables you to implement good policies, you must sometimes use tactics you dislike. If the opposition resorts to distasteful methods, you must often answer in kind or suffer defeat. If and when you are appointed, then you can do what you want and steadfastly run a clean government. But if you refuse to get your hands a little dirty during your campaign, you often never get the chance. You must decide what is more important: the reforms you wish to institute or your spotless conscience.

The other side of that coin, of course, is making certain that your actions to attain a platform do not so stain you that you become unfit to hold it. To use an extreme example, when Adolf Hitler's political party was seeking his election, it was not uncommon for his opponents to be thrown out of high windows to their deaths. The claim that the ends justify the means becomes hollow when the good you intend is overshadowed by the harm you do.

This leads us to the interesting question of what to do when the wrong person occupies a powerful platform. The epic the Mahabharata recounts the Mahabharata War, which was fought to overthrow a tyrant. Many times during the conflict, the forces opposing the tyrannical king adopted the unsavory tactics of their enemies. They lied or withheld important but inconvenient truths. They broke promises. The ones we regard as the good guys resorted to these tactics because they were fighting to replace a wicked king whose rule was harsh and unconscionable. They fought to put a better, wiser, nobler man on the throne. They fought for the platform not because they were jealous of its power, but to keep it from being abused any longer.

We know what happened when Hitler took power in Germany. We saw the horrors of his rule as his armies swept across Europe. Hitler and his allies sought to conquer nations and create the Third Reich. They were cruel rulers in every land they came to hold. All diplomatic and political means had failed to stop their aggression. Terrible, widespread war became the only remaining option if humanity was to flourish within benevolent manmade infrastructures rather than suffocate under the rule of bad people on high platforms.

Even famously pacifistic Gandhi said, "I advocate training in arms for those who believe in the method of violence. I would rather have India resort to arms in order to defend her honor than that she should in a cowardly manner become or remain a helpless witness to her own dishonor."

He possessed nonviolent means to be superior, and sought to exclusively use those attributes. Still, he recognized that while war was not a desirable answer, sometimes it was the only answer. Most modern political power struggles are undertaken with elections and other nonviolent means, but wars have always been fought to attain or strengthen a platform, and it is likely that they always will be. It seems an inevitable result of having the wrong person on the right platform.

Beyond preexisting platforms, some people create their own platforms that they use to shape our world. One could say that starting a family with a spouse is one such platform. The parents guide the family toward their particular vision of life. Parenthood is ancient, but each family is new and follows a subtly unique path. Many people create companies that they direct to success in their own way. Steve Jobs and Bill Gates created computer companies that became industry giants and changed the way we live. Gates continues to influence the world as cochair of his foundation—another self-created platform—sponsoring research in many fields, by which he hopes to benefit humanity.

Returning to George Washington, we can see that he, too, created a new platform from which he could execute a shared vision that he and his fellow revolutionaries engendered. Drawing heavily from the political genius of James Madison, the American founders developed many new structures and platforms. Let's consider Washington's rise to power in order to see the five pillars in action as he created his own platform: the presidency of the United States of America.

Born into a wealthy family in Colonial Virginia, Washington was well positioned to rise to influence, as his upbringing afforded him excellent opportunities to become familiar with leadership. He embraced the traditional role of firstborn sons (platform) by serving in the Colonial militia, gaining experience (efforts, in the form of tactics) and a good reputation (individual) that helped him become a senior officer (platform) during the French and Indian War. He led the men he commanded (means) to various victories, including a successful ambush (efforts) of a French patrol, furthering his reputation for excellence in command (individual).

While King George of England was embroiled in a war with France, the colonies saw an opportunity to take advantage of British forces being committed elsewhere, and formulated plans (efforts) to break away. Washington's renown as a strong and capable leader of soldiers (individual) became such that the Second Continental Congress commissioned him as commander in chief (platform) of the Continental Army (means). During the American Revolution, he led the Continental Army against better-trained and better-equipped (means) British forces that were formerly his allies.

In part because the progressive ideals of the Revolutionaries (individual) were so appealing to the French, and partly because they saw a tactical advantage (efforts) in keeping British forces committed on two continents, France lent significant aid to the colonists' bid for revolution. This could not have happened if

Washington had developed a reputation (individual) as cruel to captured or surrendered French soldiers during the previous war, or if he had held grudges (individual) against those he'd once battled, and refused their help out of mistrust. Either situation would have likely doomed the war effort.

When the American Revolution succeeded, as the somewhat unlikely story goes, Washington was offered a crown with which to rule as king of the newly liberated lands. Three times it was offered, and three times he rejected it. This is likely an embellishment of the truth, a type of pro-Washington propaganda (efforts). We do know that Washington held the former colonies under his military control (means) after the British forces withdrew, and he resigned his commission. In short, he stepped down instead of seizing power. This further cemented his renown as a man of honor and integrity (individual). Shortly afterward, the Electoral College unanimously elected Washington to the newly minted platform of president of the fledgling United States of America.

Washington's story has one significant omission. What help there was from the fifth pillar, the Divine, is not for me to say, and certainly is not in the history books. Given the number of opportunities a man at war—even a general—has to be killed, we may well assume there was some help from the spirit world. Even when outmaneuvered by more experienced British commanders, Washington led his forces away from defeat with far fewer losses than one might expect, keeping the Revolution alive, even in defeat. It seems clear that he was very blessed, exceptionally lucky, or both.

While we have largely discussed the pillars separately, they are very much interrelated. They are not five pillars standing detached under an open sky; each pillar jointly helps to support the positive result of an action. Whether or not a good outcome occurs greatly depends on how well each of the pillars bears it up.

Imagine you are the president of the United States. Even though you hold the same title as George Washington, the platform is significantly different because the other pillars have changed. Obviously, the second pillar (individual) isn't the same because you are a different person and bring different levels of education and understanding about our physical world. For example, the existence of dinosaurs wasn't discovered until 1858. And, while Washington's military background helped him in dealings with the armed forces, you may have more skills than Washington did in commerce, education, or other fields.

Let's consider the third pillar (means and tools). Westward expansion after Washington's term in office vastly increased the natural resources available to Americans. Likewise, new shoreline meant new naval ports and better access to a larger portion of the globe. In our time, technological advances have created staggering increases in manufacturing, food production, and transportation options. Technology we take for granted would have seemed like magic to the first president; even Benjamin Franklin would scarcely have believed modern technology possible. Suffice it to say we have far more tools and financial means at our disposal than Washington ever had.

The fourth pillar (efforts) has likewise expanded from the days of Washington. For example, we have a two-hundred-year advantage in warfare tactics and options: General Douglas MacArthur's island-hopping amphibious drives, surgical strikes by highly specialized commandos, the shock and awe of joint air strikes, and bombardments from rapid armored divisions. Classics known to Washington—such as the Fabian strategy—remain available and viable, but the paths to success have increased with the arrival of modern tools and new strategies to employ even the most classic of strategies. We can also defeat an opponent by more peaceful means through new options such as satellite surveillance and modern spycraft, made possible by changes in technology, an aspect of the third pillar.

American economic might provides us with the option of establishing a trade embargo against an opposing nation, likely leading to public pressure and dissent. Promises of financial aid or withholding money can often produce results. Inclusion in a global confederation of nations, such as NATO or the United Nations, offers still more peaceful options for addressing a problem.

Occupying the office of the president of the United States comes with many advantages and options Washington did not enjoy. Once again, the platform is strengthened by another pillar, and the results of one's efforts are more likely to be favorable.

The last pillar—call it luck, or the Divine—is harder to speak of in comparative terms. Washington's relationship with the unseen world is a matter of speculation—and yours is unknown to me. However, we can see the many ways luck or Divine forces can affect an endeavor. It may be tempting to say fate will decide, or that the dice will fall where they may. But rather than abdicate the fifth pillar, I suggest a different approach, one inspired by Krishna in ancient India.

In the Mahabharata War, Krishna served as charioteer to a mighty warrior, Arjun. Before the conflict begins, Krishna was seen giving prayers and offerings to Durga, a fierce form of mother goddess. Durga was known to be a powerful help in wartime and in efforts to prevail over evil. This assistance was exactly what Krishna and Arjun needed to succeed in the tasks that lay ahead.

Above their chariot, Krishna mounted a flag bearing the image of Hanuman—a symbol of strength, perseverance, and devotion that was meant to both inspire as well as invoke the help of Hanuman himself. Today, many view the monkey god as the patron deity of martial arts, such as grappling and acrobatics. The great ape was also the general of Ram's army in the epic the Ramayana, and his martial wisdom and experience could well have been of great use in the conflict.

I must mention that Ram, too, gave prayers and offerings before he set out to rescue his wife. This is another example of a great, legendary person not leaving the fifth pillar to chance, but seeking to bring the unseen world to his aid. Ram, facing a terrible foe, said prayers and provided offerings to the god Shiva before embarking. Only then did he believe his mission could possibly succeed.

Such examples as Krishna and Ram are instructional. Even though they had a vastly deeper connection to the unseen world than you or I do, they did not take for granted that help would come from that realm without their taking action. For many thousands of years and across all cultures, people have used prayers, chants, offerings, and talismans to bring help from the unseen world to guide them to good results. In that way they sought to strengthen the fifth pillar so it would hold firm under the weight of their goals and grant them success in their earthly endeavors.

A common misconception is that Hinduism is only about the unseen world—that the observable world is unimportant—and that Hinduism's great works, such as Bhagavad Gita, teach that results do not matter, so we shouldn't concern ourselves with them. Suggesting that results don't matter so we shouldn't seek them defies common sense. We study in hopes of passing our exam. We plan because we hope to make our lives run smoothly. We seek results in everyday activities; therefore, Hinduism is clearly about more than the unseen world.

Krishna's teachings in Gita about the five pillars are entirely about success and achieving good results, and are eminently practical. They are meant to both help us touch the unseen world with waking eyes, as well as thrive in *this* world. Results in this world do matter, and Gita's teachings exist in part to help us all achieve positive results.

Krishna was a deeply important teacher, who helped us to understand our world and our journey from life to life. He worked very hard to impart these lessons as part of his greater plan: to preserve the balance the great infrastructure requires for all of us to live and prosper in this world.

This responsibility is a sacred duty for all of us to bear, not just great teachers like Krishna. We can support the infrastructure peacefully in a quiet life. Perhaps it's our calling to build new bridges to the unseen so that we may learn more about our nature and purpose. Or we might be called on to maintain the balance through battle if the wrong person takes a powerful platform and causes great suffering, as we saw in the Mahabharata War or during World War II. Whatever platform we occupy, however seemingly unimportant, we serve ourselves best when we serve the whole and work to keep the infrastructure of our world healthy.

Whether in significant or humble ways, strengthening and preserving the infrastructures that shape and support our individual and joint journeys through life is a sacred trust. We must protect the balance of our world—our spiritual ecosystem—to ensure that we are free to further the journey of self-knowledge that we undergo from life to life.

CHAPTER 3

The Value System
of the Universe — Dharma

HINDUS HAVE LONG UNDERSTOOD THE sacred duty we all share to protect the infrastructure that allows for spiritual flourishing. The set of laws protecting our spiritual pathways, and thus protecting the greatest possible good, is called *dharma*.

Like many words, *dharma* can mean a number of things. For our purposes, think of it as the value system for our world—the *maya loka*—that helps life grow, flower, and dance. Where dharma differs most from other sets of rules and values is in its scope and origin. The US Constitution, for example, is a set of rules and values devised by the Founding Fathers in 1787 to govern their fledgling nation. Included were ideals such as a free press to keep the new government in check, and freedom of religion to prevent a state church. James Madison devised a blueprint for a strong central government composed of three branches—legislative, executive, and judicial—with separate but equal authority so one branch could not seize power at the expense of the other two. These novel ideas and others were set in place so Americans could go about their business in peace so that they might thrive.

Taking the Constitution as a metaphor, if we regard the Founding Fathers as analogous to the universal consciousness, or the Divine, and we consider Americans analogous to all of life everywhere, then we can begin to understand dharma. *Parmatma*—the source of all life—set rules and values that all life and all existence can thrive in. These rules were not set down in a document, but woven into the very fabric of our universe.

Dharma is what keeps our world in balance—and is also what *we must do* to keep our world in balance—so we can grow and thrive. There again is that notion I spoke of earlier: we are both the beneficiaries of the spiritual infrastructure and its custodians. We are responsible for its maintenance by following dharma. This is a critical point to understand.

Dharma is not a religion, philosophy, or any other sort of institution. It's more a law of nature, like physics. No one had to understand the force of gravity for it to bind our world together. No one invented dharma any more than they invented the forces driving physics. We only seek to describe these things as well as we currently comprehend them.

Dharma is as old as the universe, woven into the universal fabric to keep the world of maya running smoothly. Dharma knows no national borders; it needs to honor no treaties. It is apolitical and beyond any organized or institutionalized religion. Each attempt to create a system in which mankind may flourish starts with someone who desires to instill dharma in human society.

I don't doubt that this is done with utmost sincerity; however, we have our limits and fall short of the mark in our imitations of dharma. Basic human rights, for example, are intended to promote reasonable happiness and prosperity in people's lives. But dharma is even more important than human lives.

I understand if that statement gives you pause. Western culture in general raises its children to regard quality of life as everything—the protection of life, paramount. Systems are set up for that purpose. But are such systems really working to everyone's betterment?

Consider prisons in the United States. Street-gang members consider it a gladiator school of sorts and feel no shame in being incarcerated; it's become a rite of passage. They only emerge better criminals, taught by the older, more accomplished criminals serving life sentences. That does not seem to serve the common good.

To save court costs, prosecutors push for plea bargains, where the person accused of a crime pleads guilty in exchange for more lenient sentencing. The privatization of prisons has made the incarceration of our own citizens into an industry. It should give us pause that economics seems to be more important than justice. What abuses potentially follow from such a system?

While dharma is certainly the inspiration behind ideas such as justice and human rights, it is not about human rights, and it is not about justice. Dharma is not about the preservation of human life either. It is more important than all these things. If life is lost, life will occur again in the cycle of birth, death, and rebirth. But if dharma is not upheld and the world spirals into chaos, what good does it do anyone to be reborn? Can we do the work of living a peaceful life, pursuing self-discovery, and living in harmony with others if bandits rule the streets, despots run the statehouses, and terrorists bomb our buses? No, we cannot.

This world, the maya loka, exists to give everyone opportunities for growth and betterment, but this cannot happen if dharma is not maintained, just as crops cannot grow if the soil isn't fertile. Terrorists and despots salt the fields they claim as their own, and no growth can happen there. Therefore, such people must be struck down and plowed under to make the soil fertile again.

Much is made of nonviolence, and many think we all should be pacifists. I find that stance a grave mistake. I would argue that nonviolence is a useful tool in serving dharma. While I do not believe that violence is a virtue, I do suggest that violence is sometimes necessary to preserve dharma so that virtue can thrive.

In Sanskrit, violence (*himsa*) and nonviolence (*ahimsa*) are both tools. Worship of ahimsa spread in the country of my birth, and it made us vulnerable to foreign exploitation and enslavement in the form of colonization. This caused no end to the degradation of our national spirit and identity, and broke our parampara, the tradition of passing down knowledge. Who can say what damage the reeducation of generations has done to us spiritually?

I have found that a similar feeling about extreme ahimsa— nonviolence at any cost—has taken hold here in the West as well. I once heard a man say that he would not attack a thief who entered his home because he feels it's not worth killing or even harming someone over a television set.

I countered by asking, "Is the television all the thief would take from you?"

Would a person who entered your home with the express purpose of wronging you not also rob your family of its sense of security? Would he not steal your wife's ability to stay home alone without fear? Would your two young daughters grow up fearful that this thief might return some night with darker motives? Is this stranger's well-being somehow more valuable than your own and that of your family? The thief clearly thinks his rights and desires should come before yours, but why do you think so as well? While the philosophy of nonviolence places a high value on human life, does it do anything to defend your family or deter crimes and other attacks on them? It does not; it only serves your self-image as a peaceful person.

Buddha was famously peaceful. It's said that Buddha's peace created a zone around him where no one could harm another. This is a very clear sort of virtue. It's easy to recognize and easy to admire. Great spiritual people are often perceived to be great peacemakers. When Jesus of Nazareth spoke of turning the other cheek if one is struck, it seemed clear to everyone that this was a good man because that sort of goodness is easy to see. Nobody asked him, "But what do you do if he just keeps hitting you?"

Goodness in itself is wonderful, and nonaggression is a conspicuous trait of goodness. However, good people must also take measures to keep from being taken advantage of, slaughtered, or enslaved. Goodness has a weakness: it is easy to take advantage of someone you know will forgive you. It is also easy to harm or kill someone who refuses to fight back. That is virtue's inherent vulnerability.

When you forgive too often, it simply leaves you vulnerable to an abuser. We must not avoid taking action to prevent our own abuse because we wish to be virtuous. There is no virtue in allowing ourselves to be used and harmed; we have a duty to protect ourselves. We're not only defending ourselves, but also defending other potential victims. When we stand up for ourselves, we stand up for dharma.

Imagine for a moment what the world might be like if Hitler and his Nazis had been victorious in World War II. Prior to the Pearl Harbor attack, many Americans spoke of the beauty and worthiness of peace, adopting a "live and let live" philosophy. They argued passionately that conflict in Europe was not the United States' problem and not worth the lives of American soldiers. Ask yourself if the world would have been better off had we sat out that war.

In retrospect the answer seems obvious: a hate-mongering despot such as Hitler could not be allowed to continue. Hitler and his disciples did not care about the natural order of the world or dharma. Such men don't mind if the entire world is a heap of skulls, so long as they are left standing on top of the heap. There was never a choice. Hitler had to be removed from his platform, dharma had to be served, and those who were called had to fight. When war was declared, Americans responded. Young men enlisted in the armed forces and fought overseas against an enemy they had never met in places they had never seen.

A different version of the same thing was happening at home. American women went to work at factories and foundries. The women of this generation produced vast quantities of armaments and munitions and everything else the men overseas required. They gave up their hosiery in order to make parachutes, and the public gave up their normal foodstuffs in favor of rations. The war effort required everyone to sacrifice and do his or her part. Hindus call it *swadharma*, the duty one owes as a part of the greater whole. When we speak of each person having a duty, a job to do, or a role to play in this life, swadharma is all of those things. A soldier must fight the enemy, and a doctor must heal. If a soldier decides not to fight or a doctor chooses to do harm, the natural order is undermined. The soldier cannot allow others to be harmed because he has decided to value ahisma above his duty any more than a doctor can decide to murder a man with a deliberate overdose of medicine because he thinks the man is a bad person. We hear the rationalizations behind their actions, but is anyone really being served?

Swadharma is a person's innate potential in the life currently being lived. It may have been different in another life. Perhaps the magistrate was once a farmer—and before that, a soldier. In every life, he had a job to do. He had a swadharma, a personal duty and role to fill that served dharma. In each role, he was to serve the ultimate good. So should we all.

If we shirk this duty, we rob ourselves and everyone else of the contribution we ought to make to the betterment of all. In ignorance of dharma, that might be easy to do, but when we know what is needed from us, when we can see clearly the role we must fulfill, it becomes simpler to do what we must than to try and justify shirking our duty.

Psychologist Abraham Maslow said, "A musician must make music, an artist must paint, a poet must write if he is to be at peace with himself. What a man can be, he must be." This is swadharma. If we are to be at peace with ourselves, we must do what we are meant to do. We must fulfill our purpose.

Swadharma is not rigid, however. Our purpose can change. You can be a student at one point, then later be an attorney practicing law in a courtroom, and after a number of years be appointed a judge. In each of these stages, you have a job to do. The student must learn, the lawyer must argue his case, and the judge must make rulings. In all these roles you must do your best to fulfill your potential.

Just as water seeks the lowest point, people must seek their highest potential. Otherwise, we will be unfulfilled and shortchange the world. We must live life in accordance with our swadharma and always strive to find the highest expression of ourselves. In that way we may each play our part, and in doing so, serve dharma.

Not only do we *need* to answer our callings, we must also *be allowed* to do so. *Swatantrata*, often translated as *freedom of expression*, is an important part of dharma. We cannot seek out our highest point, the expression of ourselves that will most benefit the world, if we are murdered, enslaved, or otherwise hindered in our journey. The freedom, the ability to fulfill our purpose, must not be taken away by tyrants and terrorists. We need liberty to continue our great journey.

It can be difficult to see what dharma is. Life is not a movie with simple, black-and-white moral choices. Plus, we operate with human perceptions and within flawed human systems. Naturally, it would be risky to say that a thing serves all life when we can see so little of it. Limited by the senses of our physical bodies and swayed by our passions, we can easily go astray. We stand at risk of saying that a thing serves dharma, when in truth, it serves our desires. We often only see the difference in retrospect. Perhaps our best compass comes from listening to that connection to the Divine living in all of us. The more earnestly we endeavor, the more success we will have to act in service of dharma.

Serving dharma is not the only good or legitimate action worth taking in our lives. We don't need to judge every action in terms of how much it directly benefits the entirety of creation. We don't have to save the world from evil with our every breath. Nor do we need to remake civilization in a more perfect form each day before breakfast. Live your life with a sense of connectedness to our shared spiritual infrastructure. And if you see something you can change for the better, answer the call.

A verse in the *Manusmriti,* an ancient Sanskrit legal text, states that dharma preserves those who preserve dharma.

Perhaps we are now prepared to explore a great story of exactly this phenomenon.

Why was dharma so important to Krishna, Buddha, and others? Why was Krishna willing to be part of world war during his times to protect this value system called dharma? Is dharma the same thing as being good or doing good deeds? Or is it beyond good and bad? These are all questions to ponder, and that's why we will discuss Bhagavad Gita next—where Krishna addresses dharma, karma, and more.

CHAPTER 4

Our Calling to Preserve Dharma — Bhagavad Gita

EVERY CHILD GROWING UP IN India hears the sweeping tale known as Bhagavad Gita, or *Song of the Lord*, that recounts how a young man named Arjun comes to understand that he must answer the call to preserve dharma. We often refer to it simply as *Gita*, and everyone knows what story in song format we are talking about because it has held an important place in Hindu culture since its creation some five thousand years ago. This book has provided limitless value to me throughout my life, and much of the wisdom I hope to share with you is drawn from its pages.

Gita begins with Arjun overlooking the battlefield at the beginning of the Mahabharata War. Arjun was no holy man or pilgrim; he was a great warrior blessed with powerful weapons and cloaked in many victories. Yet he did not wish to fight.

Arjun and his four brothers, the Pandavas (sons of Pandu), stood arrayed against an army that included the Kauravas, one hundred sons of Dhritarashtra, the blind king of Kuru. Five brothers against one hundred sounds daunting, but the Pandavas were extraordinary heroes, and they were not afraid.

King Pandu was unable to produce children, but his wife, Kunti, was given the secret to having a child by whichever god she chose via a summoning ritual. She performed this ritual four times, and gave her husband four exceptional children.

Yudhishistr, the eldest son, was born of Kunti and Dharma, the god of virtue. He was moral and just in all his actions and virtuous beyond reproach. Yudhishistr was born to succeed his father as king, and was perfectly suited to the part.

Bhim, the second son, was given to Kunti by the powerful wind god, Vayu. He possessed unbounded athleticism and the strength of ten thousand bull elephants. Bhim was a warrior of tremendous ability, and the brothers relied on him most heavily in battle. The enemy rightly feared him.

Third was our hero, Arjun, born of Kunti and Indra, god of war and the sky. Arjun was a master of archery, the most highly prized fighting skill of his day. That accomplishment contributed to his popularity and made him the favorite pupil of his weapons master, Drona. Arjun was admired even by gods, and was granted the ability to use Divine weapons.

The last of Kunti's sons, Nakula, was sired by Nasatya, one of the twin gods of sunrise and sunset. Nakula was a great swordsman and diplomat, and a consummate charmer.

Kunti performed her ritual again so King Pandu's second wife, Madri, could also have a child. She summoned Dasra, the second twin god of sunrise and sunset, and the fifth Pandava brother, Sahadeva, was born. An expert swordsman like Nakula, Sahadeva was the wisest of the Pandavas. He was also the most withdrawn and mysterious.

The brothers' opponents, the soldiers of King Dhritarashtra's army, were also powerful warriors of great renown and fantastic abilities. Gita was given to us thanks to Dhritarashtra's son and advisor, Sanjay, whose ability to survey the entire battlefield with utmost clarity enabled us to know the content of conversations that occurred far from him.

The head of the Kuru army was Dhritarashtra's eldest son, Duryodhan, whose name means *unconquerable warrior*. It was Duryodhan, and not his father, who caused most of the strife between the two factions. He was jealous of Yudhishistr, the eldest Pandava and heir to the kingdom, and tricked him out of his birthright through an unfair game of dice, stripping the Pandavas of all their land and even their wives. A second game sent the brothers into exile for five years. Duryodhan was as unrelenting in his persecution of the Pandavas as he was powerful in battle.

Another member of the Kuru army was Arjun's rival and fighting equal, the dreaded Karn, who was also Duryodhan's closest friend. Unknown to the Pandavas, Karn was Kunti's secret son by the powerful sun god, Surya. Karn was perhaps the greatest of all warriors, and resented that Guru Drona taught Arjun how to use weapons and the art of fighting, but refused to teach Karn, who ached to defeat the brothers on the battlefield.

Despite their past relationship, Drona aligned with the Kuru army to fight against Arjun and his brothers. In fact, many members of the enemy's forces were Arjun's personal friends, which he found distressing, not wanting to fight his friends or his teacher. He was horrified that many of them would die, some by his own hand. And considering the champions who made up the opposing force, any one of Arjun's brothers might die, which was simply unthinkable to him.

At the beginning of Gita, we find Arjun trying to devise a way to avoid a war that would cost him terribly, whatever the outcome. Although he had been a warrior all his life, possessing fantastical weapons of vast power and an array of skills that make him a terrible force, Arjun sought to rationalize turning his back on the war and the world. He shared his thoughts on the folly of war to his longtime friend Krishna.

There are three gods in the Hindu trinity (the Trimurti): Brahma, the creator; Shiva, the destroyer of evil; and Vishnu, the preserver of good. Krishna is one of Vishnu's avatars—a god made flesh to walk among us in the maya loka. I have called Vishnu the preserver because he preserves what's right and good. He comes and defends the world when it is threatened by evil and chaos. In Gita 4:7–8, Krishna says, "Whenever righteousness wanes and unrighteousness increases, I send myself forth. For the protection of the good and for the destruction of evil, and for the establishment of righteousness, I come into being age after age."

Understand, this is how we see Krishna in retrospect. His contemporaries, like the Pandavas, only saw him as a remarkable man. Arjun valued Krishna's valor and his strategic mind. Only late in the battlefield conversation did Krishna reveal his *virat rupa,* or cosmic self, so that Arjun would know the true identity of his friend.

Krishna listened to Arjun make all the reasonable arguments against war, which were perfectly logical and correct. But none of it mattered because events that transpired before the scope of Gita made peace impossible.

At his son Duryodhan's urging and driven by his own ambitions, King Dhritarashtra was determined to wage war against the Pandava brothers. Krishna went so far as to reveal his Divinity to the king—who was granted Divine sight so he could witness the spectacle—to show that the war would be unholy and an affront to the natural order. But Duryodhan did not relent, and even conspired to imprison and humiliate Krishna while he was on his diplomatic mission to preserve the peace. King Dhritarashtra gave in to his love for his son, and the unjust war became inevitable. Duryodhan would have his war and destroy the Pandavas. When the final chance to avert war was lost, Krishna moved on to what he knew with perfect clarity must be done.

So the time for peace was done, and war was upon them, whether Arjun's heart was in it or not. Arjun was paralyzed by his unwillingness to do what must be done, but the very fact that Vishnu incarnated himself as Krishna meant that a great threat to dharma had come upon the world, and that it must be stopped.

Krishna did not show Arjun that he needed to fight in the war because fighting is virtuous for its own sake. He advocated upholding dharma. Such is the vision and clarity of mind that Krishna possessed when he spoke to Arjun on the battlefield. He knew what must be done and knew that he must teach Arjun so that he could see it clearly too.

Krishna saw with the clarity that comes from within. He knew what sort of ruler Duryodhan would be when he inherited Dhritarashtra's swollen kingdom. The seeds of tyranny were already bearing fruit within him. Someone like Duryodhan would not care about dharma, and would consider the ultimate law a nuisance to be overcome.

This is precisely why Krishna worked to keep Duryodhan from ascending to the platform of king. Dhritarashtra was neither an especially great ruler, nor particularly terrible. His failings, for the most part, involved allowing his son to do as he wished. But Duryodhan's reign would be an age of terror. He would throw all that causes life to flourish and thrive into the fire, and laugh as the world suffered. Arjun was a warrior, and as such, he had a duty to take up his weapons and stand against such a man. That was Arjun's *swadharma*, which is what Krishna helped him to see.

Some have wondered why Krishna befriended Arjun instead of Yudhishistr, the wisest Pandava and future king. On the surface, the answer is very simple: everyone else was ready to fight. Everyone else was standing up and doing what must be done, but Arjun was hanging back because of his attachments, conscience, sensitivity, and wisdom. But Krishna's choosing of Arjun went deeper than that. Arjun had already mastered the things of this world, which put him in the perfect position to move on to other things. It was the ideal time to give focus to the journey within, adding spirituality to an already fruitful life.

Plus, Arjun and Krishna had been good friends for many years. They had already fought one important war together, and Arjun had always shown a great zeal for learning. That was surely one of the reasons his weapons master, Drona, favored him so highly. Karn was certainly equal to Arjun as a warrior, yet Drona set things up in such a way for Arjun to prevail, keeping the two from competing directly. An educator in any capacity will understand the joy of teaching someone who eagerly wishes to learn. The importance of the student's readiness is hard to overstate.

Often, Indian spiritual teachings are perceived as negative and seen in terms of sacrifice. This is not the norm. There have been some rare individuals whose path moved them to turn their backs on the world to make their spiritual journey their sole focus. While that is a valid path, those hermits are not following the path that most of us should take. When Arjun—fearful for the deaths of his friends and relatives—contemplates that path in the beginning of Gita, Krishna intercedes.

Seeing his friend in despair, Krishna didn't try to change Arjun's mind about the war; instead, he worked to change Arjun's entire state of being, knowing that his mind would follow. In a conversation of seven hundred verses, Krishna educated Arjun so comprehensively that Mahatma Gandhi once called Gita his "spiritual dictionary."

While Gandhi, a great man of peace and nonviolence, did not believe the events of the Mahabharata War had actually occurred, he had great respect for the work. J. Robert Oppenheimer, who directed the Manhattan Project, which developed the atomic bomb, deeply felt the gravity of their mission and carried a copy of Gita everywhere he went.

In an interview recounting his reaction to watching the first A-bomb test in the Nevada desert, Oppenheimer said, "We waited until the blast had passed, walked out of the shelter and then it was extremely solemn. We knew the world would not be the same. A few people laughed; a few people cried. Most people were silent. I remembered the line from the Bhagavad Gita: Vishnu is trying to persuade the prince that he should do his duty, and to impress him he takes on his multi-armed form and says, 'Now I am become Death, the destroyer of worlds.' I suppose we all thought that, one way or another."

Surely, it's unlikely you or I will ever be in a position to unleash such a destructive force upon the world. Just as surely, if I did have such a choice, I would also turn to Gita. It is a light in the darkness and has helped those in crisis for five thousand years.

It is beyond the scope of this book to detail the nuances of each verse, though a happy lifetime could be spent doing so. I hope only to give you a small taste so that you have some familiarity with the important work I'm drawing from, and to also whet your appetite so that you might further investigate Gita in the future.

Seeing Arjun's unwillingness to fight, Krishna did not offer to fight in his place. He served as Arjun's charioteer, a noncombatant role. As an aside, it may be helpful to know that the war chariot, manned by a driver and an archer, was the

Black Hawk helicopter of its day, sweeping into range, raining arrows upon the enemy, and sweeping back out of harm's way.

As Arjun's chariot driver, Krishna helped Arjun, but in no way took care of all his problems for him. That was not Krishna's way. He demanded we all rise up to accept our duty and take hold of it. He did not do the work for us; he magnified our efforts to protect the rightful order of the world so that life can prosper, and goodness can thrive. This was Krishna's purpose during his time with Arjun, and shall be his purpose again when he returns, as promised.

I have heard that some people expect Krishna's return to signal an end to striving, as though he will do all the work for us and rescue us from our struggles. I have a very different understanding of who Krishna was. If Gita is any indication of his character—and I am certain that it is—then upon his return, he will make us work harder than ever before. Just as Gita is a unique spiritual text, taking place as it does on a battlefield, Krishna was a unique savior: he demanded that we save ourselves.

Krishna's entire education of Arjun on the battlefield drove toward one truth: each of us has a duty in this world, and we must act to fulfill that duty. Arjun's duty was that of a warrior, not of a hermit. To embrace that duty and take action, he had to learn many things not of this world in service to this key lesson. Krishna taught Arjun about matters of the spiritual domain that would enable him to act in the flesh.

Krishna's goal was to guide his friend toward *ek-buddhi*, or perfect clarity of mind, so Arjun could not help but come to the conclusion he'd been avoiding. Krishna was not brainwashing Arjun or leading him down some winding path to a foregone conclusion. Krishna was no puppeteer, and Arjun was no puppet. Arjun had to make his own choice, as we all must. The goal was to help Arjun achieve the clarity of mind he needed to make his difficult choice.

Krishna stood for freedom in all things. One could call that his swadharma. Krishna was born in a prison cell, and at the moment of his delivery, all the cell doors flew open, which points to what he does here in the maya loka: he helps us to be free. In the case of the war recounted in Gita, he helped Arjun to see that he must fight to defeat Duryodhan's forces so people would remain free of his tyranny.

It is of singular importance to understand that Krishna did not come to do the work *for* Arjun. He advised. He lent aid. He worked in subtle ways to amplify the man's efforts. As Arjun's charioteer, he not only drove the chariot, he also performed several minor miracles to aid his friend. In one instance, Karn shot an arrow carrying a venomous snake that would bite Arjun when the arrow struck. Krishna caused the chariot to sink into the ground far enough for the fatal blow to miss. It was a minor miracle with a major result: Arjun lived and fought on.

Could the chariot have dipped beneath the arrow's path because the ground beneath the chariot was rutted or muddy?

Perhaps that's easier to imagine, but it and other such miracles that took place on the battlefield show Krishna's intervention. This is also the truth behind why things sometimes seem to work out perfectly, against all odds.

I remember a trip my family and I made to England from Calcutta, India. A briefcase held all of our essential travel documents. Somehow, we left the briefcase on the bus we took to the airport. Calcutta is famously not a rich place, and if one leaves something on a bus, it's gone forever. Everyone knows this. Yet when we realized our mistake and returned to the bus depot, there was our briefcase, safe in the hands of a person trying to figure out how to get it back to us. You may not consider this a miracle, but my family and I saw it as a minor miracle with a major result in our lives.

There are times in everyday life when, in my mind, the Divine is certainly intervening to help a person who is on a good path. Sometimes the result will just seem like luck; you're in the right place at the right time, and the perfect opportunity arises. The fuel lasts just long enough to get to the destination. The person emerges from a terrible accident unharmed. We may think we are simply lucky when things beyond our control go our way, but I see it as more than that. As we walk along a good path and do the work of our lives, the Divine is there working with us as well. It's a common saying in India that you take one step toward parmatma, and parmatma takes a thousand steps toward you, meaning each step taken on the journey toward the Divine reduces the distance between you and God by several orders of magnitude.

This is just what we see in our story as Krishna worked miracles to protect Arjun while he fought to defeat the Kauravas, who had chosen to be the enemy of dharma. The Divine, in the form of Krishna, pulled the strings that influenced all the factors outside of Arjun's control and altered the outcome of the war. When the tide of war was turning in favor of the Pandavas, Duryodhan asked his battle commander how he could be losing despite having a vastly superior force. The commander replied it was because Arjun and his brothers had dharma on their side—and yet *still* the Kauravas continued the war!

Following are a few final points. Even when nonviolence failed and Krishna saw that war was inevitable, he worked to minimize the bloodshed by ensuring that Divine weapons—capable of mass destruction—were not used. Even in wartime, Krishna remained a champion of peace and life by favoring minimal violence over all-out destruction. In the war to wrestle the kingship from Duryodhan, many warriors died—but not entire generations, which would have occurred without Krishna's intervention.

Krishna also taught Arjun how to be at peace within himself by living as he was meant to live, which Arjun had been avoiding. He fought as a warrior not out of hatred or because he loved violence. His use of force was simply the correct tool at that time in service of dharma. Once he accepted this truth, his actions flowed not from his conflicting desires, but from his center, and his mind was at peace.

Another illustration of inner peacefulness was Krishna himself. His nature was interesting because on the surface, he seemed so unlike the archetype of the sage, holy man, or guru. Buddha, for example, was a vision of external and internal peacefulness. He walked in peace and spent his life teaching peace through self-realization. Buddha was chaste and ascetic, and is always pictured at rest.

But Krishna seemed so much more like us. He took part in warfare, and even had an army of his own. He laughed and was joyful, often playing the flute to express his happiness through music. He danced with women. It's not the usual behavior of a great spiritual teacher, and yet he was as peaceful within as Buddha. He rested in his nature, and from the center, his joy abounded, as is natural in all things. He was at peace internally, regardless of the task that may have been set before him out in the world, including taking a life to maintain dharma. It would be simple for us to mistake him as an exceptional person, as everyone—even his friend Arjun—did for many years, and not see him as a great and even Divine entity.

This internal peace is harder to see. Jains—followers of Jainism, an Indian religion that teaches a path to spiritual purity and enlightenment through disciplined nonviolence—believe that Krishna, bound by the repercussions of his actions, as we all are, had to be committed to Hell for his acts of violence in upholding dharma. Such is their love of ahimsa that they view a necessary penance as the inevitable result of any violence.

I cannot imagine this to be the case, but even they are quick to point out that Krishna cannot be touched or discomforted by Hell because of his righteousness and peaceful state of being. He accepts that his stay in Hell is a necessary squaring of accounts. I am reminded of John Milton, who wrote in *Paradise Lost,* "The mind is its own place, and in itself can make a Heaven of Hell." I picture Krishna surrounded by whatever discomforts one might imagine, sitting peacefully and playing his flute, perhaps with a small smile. But again, I fear that some misunderstand both Krishna and the true nature of maintaining dharma.

I have heard it said that a true friend will tell us an uncomfortable truth. It is easier to see Buddha's goodness because he never advises us to do something that he has told us we must not do in other circumstances. Krishna, on the other hand, is that truest of friends who tells us something we are uncomfortable hearing: gentle virtue is not always enough.

Arjun had to do the work before Krishna could aid him. If Arjun had simply ridden around the battlefield with his bow at his side, never shooting an arrow, what would have been accomplished? Maintaining dharma, preserving the world as a place where we can live and grow, takes our effort. No one, not even Krishna, will do the job of maintaining dharma for us without our participation.

If we sit on our hands, the world will fall into darkness, and the necessary freedom to make progress in our journey will be taken from us. The part of the great infrastructure we call maya loka is a self-regulating system, well suited for us all to make our journey of self-discovery, the journey from life to life. But this is only so if we step up and make it so. Like Arjun, we must clothe ourselves in our swadharma and take action, which, after all, is the heart of life itself.

To me, Gita is not just a spiritual book. It deals with great mysteries of the spiritual world, but first and foremost, it is a guide to living life. Through the teachings in Gita, Krishna is offering each of us a path to success. In the beginning of Gita, Arjun is unable to make a decision, and his friend helps him see clearly. You and I can take these lessons and use them in our own lives. If I can make decisions, follow them through without distractions, and align the unseen forces with me, surely this will lead me to the most successful life possible.

The description of Gita here is far from complete. The following questions arise: Is there more to Gita than covered in this chapter? And, if there is, should we read Gita to learn more?

In the chapters that follow, I will attempt, in my modest way, to impart many lessons to you, much as Krishna imparted those lessons to Arjun before the Mahabharata War. It's my hope that the wisdom contained within will add to your already fruitful life, and that your growing understanding will make the life you are living now even better. We all have work to do because this life and the things we do in it matter.

CHAPTER 5

Is Life an Illusion?
Maya and Ego

*M*AYA, THE WORD WE USE to describe this world we
live in, means *illusion*. What is the illusion? The answer
to that lies at the core of the Hindu worldview.

Monotheism is the belief in one powerful creator and one
creation. As it is generally understood, the creator existed
outside of time and space before he did the creating, so the
creator and creation are separate.

The classical Indian worldview is that the creator and the
creation are one, which is called *monism*. Different from the
belief that there is a single creator god standing separate from
and keeping a watchful eye over the world he has created,
monism views the Divine as part of the world and the world
as part of the Divine because they were never separate.

This brings us back to the *maya* in *maya loka,* and our original question. The illusion is that separation occurs, and we are somehow alone in the world. The illusion is that you and I are separate, unrelated individuals who have never met. The illusion is that we have only ever been human, and that we shall only ever be human, and that when this life has ended for us, we will dissipate into nothing. The illusion is that we are not connected to the center and a part of the Divine whole.

Hindus call the world we live in an illusion because the things we see here are temporary constructs. Everything around us is impermanent. Glacial movement grinds down mountains. Riverbanks swell and recede. Many of the deserts of today were the ocean beds of yesteryear. It would be easy, looking at the world around us, to believe nothing is forever—and that is another illusion. The unstable, changeable nature of our world makes it seem as insubstantial as a heat mirage when compared to the unseen world, which persists unchanging.

Think of the expression, "Life is but a dream." Expand this a little further to say life is a dream that God is having in which He's not God. In that dream, in that illusion He has created, God plays the part of a shoemaker riding a bus. He also dreams He is the bus driver. And He is a trauma nurse, the patient bleeding on the table, and the worried spouse of the patient. The dream—the illusion of this world of ours—is that you are just you and I am just me. The reality is that we are all one with the Divine, and we always have been.

I have heard people argue that if this world is only a transitory place and not the whole of reality, then surely we must be wasting our time being here. I think this is certainly false, firstly because the Divine—which is unerring in nature—has placed us here. So we *must* be where we need to be, and there must be something we are here to do. And there is. We are here to perform the work of self-realization and improvement because that work can only be done here, in this world.

I want to stress the twofold nature of our purpose here. In addition to being here for self-improvement, we are likewise here to maintain this place so others may do the work of growing and improving as well. We must be good stewards of this world, or nobody will be able to thrive. One needs the other.

A fisherman must go about gathering fish to feed his family and to sell at market in order to purchase the other necessities of life that cannot be pulled from the water. The fisherman has a second job to do as well; he must safeguard the body of water where he fishes, not only because it is his livelihood—though that is an important reason—but also because others depend on it. If he is greedy and overfishes, he will deplete the fish, and next year his family will starve, as will the families who depend upon him for their fish. What befalls one befalls the entire community.

If this fisherman were to ask us why he couldn't simply stay in his home on the shore and let the fish come to him, we might think him mad. But it's much the same argument as saying our time here is a waste, and why can't we simply awaken in unity with the Divine instead of working toward it? The answer is the same in both cases: because it simply doesn't work that way.

A person cannot achieve higher consciousness without doing the work of searching within and discovering Divine truth for himself. We can learn many lessons from one another that could guide us to those truths, but we must still come face-to-face with them before we truly know. The Sanskrit word *darshan* describes realization achieved by firsthand experience. Sometimes it's knowing God by viewing the face of God for oneself. Or it can be as simple as knowing that fire will burn you because you put your hand into the flame once before. You were aware before you burned yourself that it would burn you, but only in theory. Once you have placed your palm over the candle, however, you know beyond question. That is darshan.

Reading a manual to learn to drive a car will not provide you with darshan. Reading, while important as preparation, only gives you theory. Only the experience of actually driving the car gives you a true understanding of what it is.

This is the same with all things. One hundred books on raising a child cannot teach you how it will feel to hold your first newborn. A thousand love poems will not teach you how it feels to look back upon a life you have built with your spouse. Ten thousand essays on the nature of the soul will never fully convey what you will learn about yourself if you journey within and find your center. As clever as we are, and as magnificent as our faculties can show themselves to be, there are some things we simply cannot *think* our way around. They must be *experienced* to be known.

The *Tripura Rahasya: The Mystery Beyond the Trinity*, an ancient Sanskrit text that explores the relationship between the individual and the Supreme Cosmic Consciousness, says, "Second-hand knowledge of the Self gathered from books or gurus can never emancipate a man until its truth is rightly investigated and applied to himself; direct Realization alone will do that. Therefore, follow my advice and realize yourself, turning the mind inward." (18:89–90)

Through firsthand experience with the Divine, we come to have a knowledge that is not based on rituals and teachings. This is a personal and perfect truth. When we achieve this, when we attain darshan for ourselves, we no longer speak of what we believe. We do not have to believe it; we *know*. This is the form of knowing Krishna speaks from when he instructs Arjun.

Western philosophers have often sought to prove the existence and necessity of the Divine. René Descartes asserted that a god that is real is necessarily better than a god that is not real, and since he had defined God as being characterized by perfection, his logical conclusion was that God has to be real. Blaise Pascal undertook vigorous mental gymnastics to show that belief in God is simply a better bet than disbelief because there is more to gain by belief. If God is real, one's belief would be rewarded—and his disbelief, punished. If God is a fiction, one's belief would not buy him passage to paradise, but nor would it land him in trouble. Thus Pascal, a mathematician, deduced that belief in God just adds up to the better deal.

Indian spiritual thinkers are not much interested in these mind games, which is what philosophy comes down to. Setting up logic problems in some novel way to give us the result we desire is not important to us. Our *rishis*, our sages, were not interested in intellectually proving the existence of God. For them, the *search* for God was far more important, which is why the common translation of *darshan* as *philosophy* is incorrect.

Our scriptures are not treatises based on the thought processes of our great sages; they contain statements by those with darshan/firsthand knowledge. In this case, we are talking about firsthand experience with Divine truth. Those who speak in our writings are people who have been there, people who have personally witnessed the Divine, telling us what they know to be true. When a realized soul speaks, it is no mind game; he states the facts as he sees them in earnest.

I point out this difference in traditions between darshan and Western philosophy not to disparage the latter, but because the difference is relevant to our discussion about our business in the maya loka. There is no clever mental trick to becoming enlightened. Nor will some feat of logic allow you to shrug off all the *samskara* (baggage) you have accumulated. There are no shortcuts to the work we do in this world of illusory separation from the Divine. These things take many lifetimes of conscious effort.

I must address another concern I have with the common perception of maya loka. It is another facet of the misunderstanding that Indian spirituality is about negatives. People often speak about overcoming the illusion, release from maya loka, or release from rebirth as though this world were a prison, and they were being made to suffer simply by being alive. We must be in this world—illusory as it is—until we are perfected.

Inevitably, some people think they will simply abstain from the world and accumulate no samskara. They believe they will cleverly dodge the entire cycle and skip straight to oneness. We humans are game players by nature, blessed—and perhaps cursed as well—with great intellect. When we see a system, we immediately look for loopholes and try to find a way to beat it. Krishna says in Gita 7:3, "Out of many thousands among men, one may endeavor for perfection, and of those who have achieved perfection, hardly one knows Me in truth."

The ego and maya are intertwined concepts; the illusion is constructed of ego. When we are born, we are given names. We are all born without any identity, but the names we are given become how we think of ourselves. We develop the concept of *I*, of an individual self, and we start accumulating a range of ego around our name and sense of self.

We are born into families. Our earliest relationships are with our father and mother. They are our first and most vital support system, and on some nonverbal level, we understand that we belong to one another. We are theirs, and they are ours. This is our first social awareness, and it becomes a foundation of our ego, our sense of self. Many of us have siblings, and as we interact with these siblings, we develop close and important relationships with them, whether we think they are important or not. Our immediate family becomes our initial and most critical social network. It becomes part of our identity. We think of ourselves as part of this group, which is the first of many groups we will add to a growing complex that describes who we think we are.

Later, we leave home to begin attending college. We start to recognize ourselves as a part of another group: a class. Likewise, we identify as a part of the school as a whole. As we develop new friendships in these early school years, we bond with peers who are outside of our home. These are not family members, but they become yet another discrete group within the larger groups of school and class.

In time, we progress to higher grades and higher-level schools. We participate in sports teams or hobby clubs, and our complex of ego—whom we see ourselves as—grows. Some groups will fall away. A summer friendship will pass with the coming school year. A new sports team will replace the old one, and so on. Perhaps our friends move or our family relocates, and ties to a certain group or place are severed. In some cases, we cling to these groups and continue to consider them part of our identity for decades.

I spent a year in eighth grade in Bangalore, far from my previous school in Ara. After only that single year, we moved away from there, but I had developed a deep attachment to the city and to some of my schoolmates. For many years afterward, I fondly imagined that one day I would meet those friends again, perhaps somewhere in Timbuktu, and I enjoyed imagining what a good time we would have together. I still cherish those relationships and memories. In my heart, part of me still sees myself as a boy who lived in Bangalore and as a part of those lost friendships.

When you leave your home and go off to college, your home is still your home. It remains so for many years, and that attachment will likely persist throughout your lifetime. When you leave your first schools, your attachment is likely to be less intense. It may simply become a place you used to attend. How strong those attachments remain depends on the relationships you had there.

When you finish high school and go to college, you find new friends, new living spaces, and perhaps hundreds of new classmates each term. You start to form many new attachments and begin seeing yourself in a number of new ways. You'll identify yourself by your field of study: "I'm pre-med." You'll identify as a 4.0 student, which is how your parents will proudly refer to you when they speak to their peers. You may become part of a particular dormitory, or fraternity, or sports team. You might belong to a club on campus or a study group, or be a student of Professor So-and-So. All your groups and accomplishments become part of your ego complex.

In time, you'll join the workforce, perhaps with a corporation, a nonprofit foundation, or a small business. Perhaps you'll leave for work opportunities in another country. By that point you've left behind the house you grew up in, your K–12 schools, your university, and now your country of origin. But you still probably call that original town and that original nation your home. I've met people who tell me where they live now and then add, "But originally, I'm from New York," or some other state, because that part of their self-image is so strong. It's a vital part of their ego system. Similarly, the attachment to a person's university often persists decades after commencement, and military veterans continue to identify themselves as such long after their service has ended: "Once a Marine, always a Marine."

Over the course of your lifetime, you've created a network of ego around you. So has everyone else. Meanwhile, the trees grow, the rivers flow, the sun shines, and the birds chirp. The natural world is untouched by ego and could not conceive of a network of ego. You and I are a different story. We build and modify this network of the ego, this shifting perception of self, of the identity of *I*.

When a person dies, his carefully constructed network suddenly disappears. And while that individual has left us, we still keep our relationship with him alive. My own father is dead, so his subjective world is gone. Yet surviving family members cling to their loved one with a network of ego. That attachment is a huge part of our identity.

The person is born again and starts building a fresh, new network, unaware of the previous attachments that made up his former ego system. Our complex nature includes a mechanism whereby the ego network of one life is not carried at a conscious level to the next life. Krishna says of this: "You and I have passed through many births, Arjun. You have forgotten, but I remember them all." (Gita 4:5)

The network of ego exists not only at the individual level, but also on a group scale. For example, I used to live in a small village in India named Balbandh. Looking at it from the outside as I do now, the ego system of my village is fascinating to me. The village had sections called *tolas*. People from these different tolas were—and to some extent remain—ready to feud to the point of violence over trivial matters. They were willing to kill one another over almost nothing at all. They're not wealthy, but are very rich in the collection of their ego. Their group sense of self is fierce. I understand this to be the case in many impoverished areas here in the United States as well.

Let me make it clear that I am not saying the ego system and value system of these tolas are bad or good. I am only commenting on what I see. Once you have some distance, you can see the network as a whole, and from that perspective, you can still live within the framework of that network, but a certain clarity will come to you that was impossible from the inside. We shall examine that clarity further as we continue our discussion.

Let us say you log on to the internet, use it for whatever purpose, and then switch the computer off. The virtual space is still there. Millions or perhaps billions of people are accessing it and using it at any given moment. But you can still be outside of it. The network of ego can be considered similarly. The question is, can you stand outside of this network?

With the knowledge I gleaned from Gita, and the clarity of mind granted by a lifetime of meditative practice, I can do so most of the time. Similarly, when I go to my village now and see people in tolas arguing and consumed by things I see as petty matters, I can only smile. I mean that in no way as an insult to them. I grew up with them. They contributed to who I am today. I have many pleasant memories of my child-hood there. But my horizons have widened. I have seen more of the world, and that has changed my perspective. I am not as involved as they are. Not any longer.

The smallness of the social ego system is a bit like air pollution. If you are standing within it, you cannot see it because it is all around you. You have to be standing outside of it to be able to see it. You have to see where the borders are to know that there is something else: another way for things to be. Once you have stood outside and looked in, you will have achieved darshan.

Krishna is always standing outside of the network of ego. His perspective sees the entire picture, beyond our own little ego systems. If you are inside a house and look through a window on the eastern side, you can see the sun rising, while if you look from a window on the western side, you can see only shadows. Krishna is standing outside the house, on the peak of the nearby mountain, and he can smile on what he sees. Over the course of their battlefield conversation, Krishna called for Arjun to leave the house and join him on the peak. We should similarly attempt to step outside our ego networks to see the bigger picture.

Who we think we are is informed by our ego systems. Likewise, ego governs how we relate to the world around us. Our accumulated relationships and accomplishments tell us how we must be. But it is all illusion. The king and the shepherd are equally a part of the Divine, joined at the center, though perhaps unaware of it. In the process of developing a network of ego systems, we have forgotten there is a center in all of us. We have shifted completely to the periphery, and are spending our lives only in that space. Maya loka, and thus ego, are nothing but an infrastructure that supports our development during our journey from life to death—and sometimes beyond.

Ego is helpful in the endeavors of this world. We must form these networks to conduct our daily lives. Even the most basic unit of ego, a person's given name, is an illusion. It's temporary; it was not our name before, and in some number of years, it will not be our name any longer. You could call our names a polite fiction. Yet what would we do without our names? We would have great difficulty communicating with one another. How would our mothers, our teachers, and our coworkers go about getting our attention or discussing us with one another? Yes, all of ego is a necessary fiction, helpful to us in moving about and being a part of this world. We need our identity to take part and perform our duties here.

Conversely, ego proves to be an obstacle in the world of spirituality. We need to drop our ego, along with the rest of our attachments, when we are ready to go deeper toward the center. Naturally, some questions begin to arise: If ego is so important, how can it be bad? Why do we always talk about dropping ego? Why do we emphasize renunciation and self-lessness so much?

Words have limitations, and I have limits of my own in expressing what I know. If I say it is essential to develop ego to be able to drop it later, a selfish, willful son may tell his father, "I am in the stage of developing my ego. What is wrong with that? I will drop it one day when I am ready." Certainly, there is a truth to this. To be able to drop something, you must have it in the first place. But is that an excuse for base selfishness? Of course it is not. Remembering that humans are game players, we can see how smart people will twist these words around to find a meaning that suits them.

It is critical that we try to understand these concepts. If someone views these concepts too simply, they might say that your ego is bad and advise you to abandon your ego, even before it's fully developed, so that you are a productive part of this world. Where would that leave you? No place you'd probably want to be, and I doubt you would thank this person for it. Let's not say that ego is bad. Ego is a useful fiction; use it, but don't be deceived by it.

The day will come when it's time to step back from ego and see the bigger picture. At this point in our development— once we have created a life for ourself and can be a productive member of our society—we may then add to this life by looking beyond it. That's when we join Krishna and Arjun on that mountaintop, look down upon our smallness, and devote ourself to finding the center.

If you dive deep into yourself, you'll find that your name has disappeared. The very idea of self has disappeared. What you find instead is pure existence beyond the fiction, beyond the striving. As you journey toward the center, you find pure being within, which is not separate. It is not yours or mine because it is *ours*. This type of being is all-inclusive. It excludes nothing; rocks, rivers, mountains, and trees are all included. The whole past, the whole future—everything in this immense universe is part of the Divine whole, common to all.

The deeper you journey into yourself, the more you will find that separate identities don't exist. Individuals don't exist. What exists is a pure universality. On the circumference we have names, egos, identities. When we jump from the circumference toward the center, all those identities disappear. What remains is *atma*, the center of all—the universal soul.

Once you have made the journey inward to the center, you can return to your ordinary life here in the maya loka, but you will be qualitatively different. Your state of being will be altered. Returning to the periphery, you will still use your name and the entire ego system you had gathered before, but you'll find a qualitative difference in yourself and in your interactions with the world.

I'm reminded of the parable of the ten bulls, which is a metaphor for the journey to self-realization and the evolution of awakening. In the story, a boy is out in the pasture looking for a lost bull, which represents self-nature. It was never lost; only ignorance kept the boy from seeing it. Eventually the boy finds tracks leading to the bull, which represent the teachings that can help us find our inner truth. The story continues with the boy catching sight of the bull, wrestling with it, and finally managing to tame it. It's an analogy of the great struggle to tame the unruly mind and at last become mindfully connected with our center, our atma. After the boy achieves a new state of being, his journey is not complete until he comes full circle and returns to the world from which he came.

When the boy leads the bull home, the bull that returns is different because it has been tamed, and the boy is also different for having done the work to tame it. Now walking the same paths he knew before, the boy sees the world differently, and his former cares mean nothing to him. He is still living and working in the world, but is now full of the bliss that comes from connectedness to this true nature. He walks among men ennobled, and his presence is ennobling to those he meets. He is the same boy, with the same name, living in the same town, but now everything is different because he has created a conscious connection to atma.

CHAPTER 6

The Ultimate Connection — Atma and Parmatma

JOIN ME IN PICTURING A beautiful lotus flower. It has a golden-hued center surrounded by an array of delicate petals, ring after ring of them extending outward like ripples in a pond. These rings of soft-colored petals extend as far as the eye can see—and farther. Picture this with me.

Now we shall label the parts of this infinite flower to illustrate our topic for this chapter. The golden central hub is *parmatma*. It is the center of all centers and the pool of consciousness from which all souls arise. Perhaps no one can say when or why a soul is issued into one of the rings from the center, but that soul, or *atma*, remains attached to the flower's center. While we may imagine each petal as a separate entity, that's *maya*, an illusion. Separation from the center is only a trick of the mind.

When the Divine center—parmatma—produces another petal (atma), it is not diminished. The *Ishavasya Upanishad* speaks of a formula expressing this concept: "Aum. That is the whole. This is the whole. From wholeness emerges wholeness. Wholeness coming from wholeness. Wholeness still remains."

It's far easier to understand this concept in terms of arithmetic. Infinity plus infinity equals infinity, and infinity minus infinity equals infinity. Once again, the important thing to realize is that atma is not removed from the center so much as it's differently expressed. Otherwise, the soul would seem to be changeable or impermanent. Things that have beginnings likewise have ends.

The whole of existence can be divided into two natures: *sat* and *asat*. Everything is either sat in nature (unchanging and undying) or asat in nature (ever-changing and fleeting). Our world, our bodies, everything we see and sense is an illusion born of atma.

All of maya loka, this world of illusion, is asat—impermanent. We know this already. We learned it, though perhaps not in those terms, when we first encountered death, or when a friend moved away or we experienced some other loss. This world is ever-changing. This world and everything in it is asat.

Why is this concept so real to some people, the people who know both the worlds, the world of sat and the world of asat (i.e., the maya loka)? We only know the maya loka, and as long as we are here, we only know the reality of this loka. But, if we consider that we're here for only eighty to one hundred years out of thousands of years of our life, things are not so clear. When the sat—which exists, although outside of our existence—becomes our knowledge and experience, the fleeting moments of eighty to one hundred years will look like an illusion indeed. We have just known our soul, the soul that spends a short time in the impermanent physical body.

I am fascinated by the story of a Zen master as described in a book called *Zhuangzi:*

> Once upon a *time*, I, Zhuang Zhou, dreamt I was a *butterfly*, fluttering hither and thither, to all intents and purposes a butterfly. I was conscious only of my *happiness* as a butterfly, unaware that I was Zhou. Soon I awaked, and there I was, veritably myself again. Now I do not *know* whether I was then a *man* dreaming I was a butterfly, or whether I am now a butterfly, dreaming I am a man.

It's often said that people like Zhuang Zhou don't dream; this dream description was a means of communicating his message to his disciples. The limitations of the man dreaming to be a butterfly, versus a butterfly dreaming of being Zhuang Zhou, is a limitation of the world of asat. The span of view is limited from the world of asat when compared to the world of sat.

The soul, an entity of the world of sat, has no beginning or ending. The soul is sat, permanent and unalterable. Living in maya loka can make it difficult to contemplate what that means. We have no point of reference for it. Science has taught us that even things that seem vast and unalterable to our eyes have beginnings and ends. However, consider the words of Krishna to Arjun: "Never was there a time when I did not exist, or you, or all these kings; nor in the future shall any of us cease to be." (Gita 2:12)

We may imagine the impact of these words upon Arjun, paralyzed by despair at the thought of his beloved friends and relations dying. Unlike the bodies of his friends and brothers, which were changing throughout their lives right before Arjun's eyes, there was another, unseen part of them—their soul, or atma—that would never change or be destroyed.

We are all familiar with the impermanence of the physical body. But not everyone understands that once the physical body dies, the astral body with all its samskara (baggage) travels through the incorporeal world, and then at an opportune time, enters another physical body. Thus the journey from life to life continues in its cycle.

Atma is not involved in the process of this journey; it's a catalyst. The body may have no ability to sense it, and our sciences may be unable to detect its presence, but atma is here within us all. Atma is connected directly to the parmatma, the universal supreme soul, and unites each of us to it, just as the base of the lotus petal connects each seemingly individual petal to the center of the flower. Otherwise, this journey we are all undertaking would not be possible.

As I write this, it is January in Maine, and the ground outside my home is frozen and covered with snow. By May, the snow will melt, and the sun will shine. The grass that grows and the flowers that bloom are not aware of the process that enables their existence; it just *is*. Atma's role in us having a physical body in this world is very similar. Whether we are aware of it or not, or can understand it intellectually or not, atma is simply there at our core. The process of life coming to be and the cycle of lives launching is a reaction to the presence of atma.

Desire and result at this level are not separate. Atma desires to get lost, and it is lost. It desires to find itself, a body is manifested, and our journey from life to life begins.

The main difficulty in understanding atma is that we think of ourselves in terms of *I* or *me*. *I* am not truly the physical body, *I* am not the etheric body, and *I* am not the astral body. Nor am *I* atma. *I* is a part of the ego, so it is maya and has nothing to do with atma. Ego is asat (impermanent), and atma is sat (eternal). Once we set aside the notion that atma is a part of our true selves and regard atma as existence itself, we get closer to the truth.

Having explained that atma is indestructible, whether by blade, fire, or flood, to put Arjun's mind at rest and ease his fear of death, Krishna impressed upon him that the perishable part of his loved ones will change, but that which is eternal will endure, whatever the outcome of the war. "For the soul, there is never birth, nor is there any death. That is unborn, eternal, ever-existing, undying, and primeval. That does not die with the death of the body." (Gita 2:20)

Krishna also posed a hypothetical situation: Even if atma were destructible, there would still be no reason to fear. If something can die, it will. And if it is going to die anyway, then it is just a matter of time until it does, and what good would it be to deny your sacred duty in the hopes of postponing the inevitable?

We all can take comfort from that lesson as well. Those loved ones we have lost are not truly lost. That which was enduring in them lives on as it always has. Only the temporary form that their atma constructed for them, the illusion, has passed away. The same will happen to us someday when it's time to move into the next stage of our journey. Our soul endures, unchanged, for all time—good deeds don't improve it; selfish actions don't tarnish it—regardless of what stage in the cycle of birth and rebirth we're in.

In the Hindu worldview, we cannot lose our soul. It is perfect and eternal, as we'd expect, knowing its origin in parmatma. That said, we may stray from our soul out of ignorance. Just as Arjun's ignorance of his true nature led to suffering as he struggled with his dilemma, many of us spin around the periphery, searching for meaning in the ephemera because we don't understand what's at our center.

Those ignorant of their nature will attempt to achieve immortality through conquest, legacy, or fame. But since it's not possible to find anything lasting in illusion, those efforts ultimately only serve to assuage the ego. We will live on while atma sheds the material body, just as we discard clothes that have worn out; they've served their purpose, and now we're done with them. Likewise, atma does not mourn dropping the material body that it created for its own purpose.

That said, Krishna was not claiming the body is unimportant. He was simply pointing out that the physical body has certain properties while atma has others, and together they share an important relationship. Consider a light bulb, which won't work if there isn't an electrical current running through it. At the same time, even if there is electricity, there will be no light without the bulb because the electricity needs a conduit. The light bulb is required for the electricity to manifest into light. In the same way, the body is required for the atma to manifest in its full glory. We have just learned that the Divine, parmatma, expresses itself through the seemingly individual soul, atma. Likewise, atma expresses itself by doing work via a physical body.

We might not understand parmatma so well had Krishna, Ram, Buddha, and Nanak not manifested in the flesh to guide us. The physical bodies of these great ones who brimmed with knowledge and power to share served important purposes, and so do ours. We all have duties in this world and parts we must play, just as Arjun had to play his part.

Trying to understand atma and parmatma raises some familiar questions: Can these concepts be understood intellectually? What's the best way to experience them? I plan to discuss techniques for doing so in a future book.

It's important that Duryodhan chose war. Even when Krishna showed his Divine form to the Kaurava leadership in hopes of averting the conflict, they made the disastrous choice to proceed. But it was their choice to make, just as it was ultimately Arjun's choice whether or not to fight. Such choices in life are always ours to make. Like Arjun, we will only find peace and happiness once we embrace our true nature instead of resisting it. As we all do, Arjun had a duty to fulfill. He just needed to discover it.

Having gained clarity about his personal duty, or swadharma, Arjun had to act on it. Just as we cannot prosecute people for their thoughts, no matter how ugly, we can't applaud them for merely thinking virtuously. They must take virtuous action to have any effect. While our thoughts do matter, for us to perform our duty and continue on our journey, we need to act. Just as our thoughts sometimes have consequences of their own—both good and bad—so do our actions, which carry much more weight.

CHAPTER 7

The Power of Karma

IN ITS COMMON USAGE, KARMA is referred to as a cosmic ledger for reward or punishment, based upon one's actions. Good karma holds the promise of positive things in the future, and bad karma portends trouble. However, I find this conventional wisdom an unhelpful oversimplification at best.

To the spiritual pioneers who originally coined the term, karma means *action*. So it's not the reward/punishment; it's the action itself. Therefore, you may hear it often said that a person is pursuing their swadharma by doing a karma.

Karma is at the center of Krishna's teachings in Gita. He presents it as pivotal in our lives and essential to our journey from life to life. Karma is a great and sweeping truth of the universe. It is intrinsic to the infrastructure of life and the systems governing our journey. Karma is not merely a byproduct of human life or limited to humans; it is cosmic. Karmas are the means by which the spiritual infrastructure is maintained. They propel us along our life's path.

The entire universe is eternally in motion. This action, this work being done, is karma in one form or another. We don't perceive it that way because our thinking is so bound by the attachment to ego. Grass grows, tree branches bend in the wind, and water erodes the hillside. All of this is work. All of this is action. It's hard for us to understand that this is karma because we see action, but no actor. We know that grass is growing, but we don't see its growth as work being done. It's merely something that happens. We consider mowing the lawn to keep it tidy to be work. In truth, the entire universe is alive with forces and systems acting upon one another even though we don't see an actor for all that action.

In Gita, Krishna draws a distinction between karma and *akarma*. Some people incorrectly translate akarma as *inaction*, but there's no precise English translation for the concept of akarma. One way to explain it would be *inaction in action*. A thing is done, but there's no one behind the action. Take, for example, rain falling. It simply rains; this action just happens. According to Krishna, this is akarma.

Humans often anthropomorphize inanimate objects; in that way, we see an actor exercising agency. The weather changes because today it cannot *make up its mind*. Creating the notion of a rain god ascribes the action to an entity, so we more easily see karmas being performed. A better method would be to understand that some actions are performed without a personality owning the action; that is *akarma*.

Examples of akarma can be seen all around us. Gravity pulls objects toward one another. Electrical current rushes through a conductive material. Sound waves vibrate through matter, radio waves travel through space, and light bends and splinters as it enters a prism. In all of these cases, work is clearly being done, karmas are being performed, but there is no one performing them. As we inhale, *prana* (life energy) flows in and out of us just as surely as oxygen and carbon dioxide are exchanged, but it's not something we control.

There is an immeasurable amount of activity, work, and energy all around us on a cosmic scale. From the movements within an atom's electron cloud to the sweep of a spiral galaxy's arms, karmas are an indivisible part of reality. Action, movement, and change are the heartbeat of the universe.

In Gita, Krishna explains how this translates into karma and akarma for you and me. If Arjun thinks he is going to fight or he is not going to fight, he is the doer in both instances. Krishna advised Arjun to take himself out of the equation and leave no doer. Krishna showed Arjun—and us—how to become like a cloud. Let the rain fall because the cloud is full, but take no credit.

Easier said than done.

Naturally, one wonders, *How is this possible and why should Arjun or I do this?* Let me ask you: Have you looked at a painter with a brush in his hand? At times, it appears that the painter is not even there. His entire consciousness is lost in his painting, and your own attention is drawn there as well. He has become the painting, and you, as a witness, fall into it also. Only when an artist's ego falls away and he loses himself in the act of creation does he tap into something universal and produce his best work. The same is true for musicians and dancers. Their best performances come out of their losing themselves in their art.

I am a surgeon, and I can tell you there is a long road to becoming a good surgeon. Surgical techniques have moved on to robotic surgery now, where the tools are no longer directly in our hands. A surgeon sits in the corner of the operating room, or even just outside the room, to perform the surgery. It's common knowledge that robotic surgery has a long learning curve, so becoming proficient requires a lot of effort, training, and practice.

That stage of my training reminded me of a question Arjun asked: How could he control his mind, which was always wandering? Krishna's answer was: "Practice, Arjun, practice."

Since I continued to practice with robotic instruments, it's now second nature for me. Once I'm on the robot, it just moves.

I know the plan, and each step of the surgery just flows from the last. Anatomical differences among patients don't present a real challenge anymore. This is not only true for me, but for all those surgeons who have trained and practiced. The surgery is no longer karma; it's become akarma. There is no doership anymore, just simply doing.

I would like to share another recent experience with you that I think will nicely illustrate akarma. I have a good friend, Lindon Brown, who enjoys skeet shooting. I was intrigued by this pastime and decided I wanted to try it myself. Lindon was delighted to see my interest, so we packed his guns in his big van and headed out to his town's skeet club. After we completed the necessary formalities, we took our positions on the field.

He gave me safety instructions and then talked me through the basics of shooting. I pulled on his command, and a clay pigeon came flying out. Lindon raised his gun, followed the skeet, and pulled the trigger. As you may have guessed, his aim was accurate, and he hit the clay. His shooting was effortless and flawless; he had practiced to a point where he did not seem to exert more effort in shooting than he would simply standing there in the field. It was just majestic to watch him do that. I could launch two clays, see them fly out, and his gun simply followed as though some invisible thread attached them. He pulled the trigger and struck the targets as though there were no other possible outcome.

Although I was an eager student, I did not have the same success. For him, it was second nature, but when my turn came, I had so much to think about! I had to figure out where to rest the gun against my shoulder, which eye to close, how to aim, and so on. By the time I had made all those decisions, the clay was completely out of sight. Again, Krishna's words "Abhyase na tu kaunteya" came to mind, and I knew the wisdom in them.

Let us explore for a moment the purpose behind actions. As much as anything else, one might say that what sets humans apart from other forms of life is that we always have these questions on our lips: "Why? What is the purpose of that?" We always want to know what a thing is for. What purpose can it possibly serve? Let us ask those questions now about some familiar akarmas. Why does a cloud dispense rain? How does this serve it? Why does the grass grow? What does it want? These questions don't sound sensible to most of us. We don't even ask these questions about a tsunami or a hurricane. We wouldn't think to do so. Perhaps this is because we are busy trying to create early warning systems to minimize the damage, so philosophy is put on hold.

When you, I, or another person does something, we want to know why it was done and for what purpose. Few people would criticize robotic surgery; it saves lives, so its purpose is evident. Someone once asked Tulsidas why he wrote the saga *Ramcharitmanas*. He responded that he wrote it for his sheer pleasure. I have seen the expression of satisfaction and happiness on the face of a skilled robotic surgeon who has successfully completed a lifesaving surgery, so perhaps that ought to be sufficient.

Be it robotic surgery, or an artist creating a painting, or a gun enthusiast shooting skeet, the doer in each case is actively involved in a specific karma he or she wants to master. Once that individual becomes an expert, karma can transform into akarma, an effortless effort, like deep-water fish that create no ripples on the surface as they swim.

However, many karmas do disrupt the water—for good and for ill—and we carry a consequence of those actions with us on our journey. This is a critical point to understand: akarma does not produce lasting, real-life repercussions; karma where doership is strong may produce lasting ripples.

Using a gun recreationally or competitively for skeet shooting is a benign action. Krishna does not discourage competition. Arjun was the best archer of his time—although he never competed against Karn—and Draupadi became his wife as a result of his win in an archery competition. No harm came from his pastime. But if the purpose of skeet shooting moves away from simple recreation to training to hunt birds, that motivation changes the entire perspective because potential harm will come to a living creature. Now imagine that someone is shooting skeet as preparation for committing a robbery or a terror attack, with the moving targets standing in for fleeing people, similar to how the al-Qaida pilots on 9/11 learned to fly planes in legitimate flight schools designed to teach people a hobby or career skill. Krishna calls these twisted actions *vikarma,* and they have consequences.

The idea that action and consequences are all bound together in this way can give us pause because there is an implicit responsibility there. Some people may grow fearful of that responsibility, and decide to withdraw from the world and stop affecting anyone or anything else. Besides being effectively impossible, it would not be their true path. Karma is not optional. As beings with material bodies, our nature is to take action. We cannot avoid doing the wrong thing by refusing to act. Indecision is not inaction; it only delays what must inevitably be done. Refusing to do your duty in essence pushes that duty onto the shoulders of another, hoping they will take the action in your stead. Of course, not all of our actions are entirely under our control. We have autonomic functions, such as breathing and the beating of our heart. We can control these somewhat if we give them our attention, but the moment we cease to think about them, they continue on as before. The unconscious actions that regulate our bodies and keep us alive are not our concern here. Karma, as we discuss it now, relates to acts that are manifestations of our mind.

It is said that all it takes for evil to flourish is for good men to do nothing, and that would certainly have been the case if Arjun had decided not to act and fight. Despite his fears for friends and relatives, Krishna taught him that he could not simply shrug off his duty and let Bhim and his other brothers do all the fighting. Without Arjun doing his karma of fighting to preserve the dharma, Duryodhan would have won the war and dharma would have been materially damaged by his cruel reign.

Whether Arjun participated or not, the war was happening, and deaths were unavoidable. That was the price to be paid for the decisions the Kauravas had willfully undertaken. Krishna, who could visualize the future, saw the tsunami of destruction the Mahabharata War would bring, including the Kauravas' deaths. Krishna said he killed them—in the sense that he represented the Divine—to preserve dharma. Arjun was just the instrument (*nimitta-matram*) of the deaths those on the Kaurava side brought upon themselves, just as the cloud is the instrument of rainwater's return to the ocean. Arjun was blameless for the karmas he undertook on the battlefield because he wasn't their author, only the medium, but the credit for victory was laid at his feet. Rather than the dishonor he feared as a result of accepting his role in the war, Arjun ended up ennobled.

His lesson on the importance of taking action applies to us all. Krishna says, "There is no one who can remain without action, even for a moment. Indeed, all beings are compelled to act by their qualities born of material nature." (Gita 3:5)

The qualities Krishna mentions are goodness (*sattva*), passion (*rajas*), and darkness (*tamas*), which are called the three *gunas*, or tendencies. All three are present in everyone and everything, but in differing proportions, influencing our behaviors and driving our karmas.

The mind has a will, and that will is carried out by our bodies. We think to take an action, and our hands do the work. This is what our bodies are for. We think to speak, and our lips and tongues create the words we use to express what's in our minds. These actions have consequences, however great or small. They ripple outward through maya loka and sometimes continue past our present lives.

There's an anecdote about Buddha stubbing his toe on a stone in the road. The toe throbbed in pain and began to bleed. To the surprise of those walking with him, Buddha expressed great relief and thanked the stone, explaining that it was the last of his karma coming back to him.

While we don't know what action of Buddha's set that stone in the road, like Krishna, Buddha could see farther in time than the rest of us. Having perfect clarity and knowledge of past lives, he could see the chain of causality that tied him to that stone and was relieved to have shaken off that chain at last.

Not all actions chain us to the results, and even those that do come with chains don't all have the same weight. A chain of iron is heavier than a chain of straw, and so it is with the repercussions of our karmas. The chain we bear for taking a life will weigh more than the chain for telling a white lie. But each is still a chain, and in time, it must be cast off.

This raises the question of what actions cause these consequences, these chains that tie us to them, while other actions leave us unbound. We have spoken about akarma, the actions that simply flow out of necessity and require no doership. By default, akarma does not create any ripples, consequences, or karmic chains. Vikarma will assuredly create ripples, consequences, and chains. These karmas are attached to desires and results, and we carry the resulting chains with us from life to life; they tie us to karmas we have done before, and we will not be rid of them until the world brings them back around to us and gives us the chance to be free of them.

CHAPTER 8

Carrying Our Baggage — Samskara

AN EXPERIENCE, A LESSON, OR the weight of a past deed—anything collected over the course of a life—can be carried on beyond death and into another life through samskaras. You can think of samskaras as a kind of baggage because they are carried with us on our journey from life to life, and like a suitcase we take on a trip, samskaras have both weight and value. But a more apt general meaning of samskara is the impressions, impacts, or imprints left on the unconscious by our actions. It can be a thing learned, a deed done, or anything that we might consider to be a part of our history. We don't need to be aware it's there, but it remains with us and helps to make us who we are in a given physical incarnation.

If you look at the word's etymology, *sam* in Sanskrit translates to *well planned*, and *skara* is *action taken*. So the word roughly means something like *planned action*, and that is at the heart of samskaras. We have discussed that intent to do an action is bound up with the doing of it—as well as the action's ramifications—in the word *karma*. With samskaras, an intentional action—one that was planned—is likely to result in a stronger samskara than one that merely occurs without thinking.

With this in mind, we can explore three contextual meanings of samskara. The first is the spirit—or soul—of a group (a nation, a religion, an ethnicity), which gives each a unique character. Consider India. The soil of India has become charged with the energy that has seeped into it from Divine entities, like Ram, Krishna, Buddha, Mahavir, and Nanak. This has created an energy field that is unique to India and found no place else on Earth. This is not said to exclude anyone. You, too, can be a part of it, and have the character of a place flow through you and become a part of your own personal story regardless of whether you were born there or not.

Let me also say that this native spirit or flavor is not a phenomenon exclusive to India. I spoke with a man who traveled to Scotland, and upon his return, he could scarcely describe what he had experienced there. The clarity and color of the water were unique to Scotland. The charge in the air was likewise unique to that place. If only you could bottle a little bit of that air and include it in a tourist pamphlet, he joked, there would be no need to say another word to get people on a plane. He did not know it, but he was speaking of the samskara of that place, this rugged nation steeped in its own history and culture. This is what created the impression upon him, just as much as any natural feature of the land. It resonates in the fabric of a place, and while you may not have words for it, the place breathes its story to you. Perhaps this is sufficient to describe this meaning of samskara.

The second contextual meaning of samskara is a sacrament or rite—celebrated in both the home and the temple—to mark our sacred spiritual journey on Earth by commemorating life milestones that are carried forward with us and influence our story. While we are in maya loka, ripening our ego and setting about to do our important karmas, there are certain milestones in our lives. Every culture consecrates the milestones of life with ritual and festivity. In India, these rites of passage—also called samskaras—are celebrated in the home and in the temple, marking our spiritual journey on Earth. Hindus celebrate life's crucial junctures with sacraments, which impress the subconscious mind, inspire family and community sharing, and invoke the gods' blessings.

Family and friends draw near, lending support, advice, and encouragement. Through ancient rites, family members or priests petition the gods for protection at important turning points, praying for the individual's spiritual and social development.

Each sacrament, properly observed, empowers normal and spiritual life and preserves Hindu culture as the soul consciously accepts each successive discovery and duty in the order of God's creation. There are sixteen popular samskaras, including the rites of conception, hair parting, birth, name giving, first feeding, the three-month blessing, head shaving, ear piercing, first learning, puberty, returning home, marriage, elders' vows, retirement, sense of self and awareness of the life lived, and last rites.

The third type of samskara refers to the remnants of our actions that we carry from one life to another. Everything we have learned, the actions we have taken, all the bodily experiences of our lives leave impressions that do not perish with our physical bodies. These impressions, or samskaras, transfer with us. After death, our astral body departs, taking all the samskaras—karma chains, emotions, attachments—which will force a new birth to occur in order for us to continue our journey. And when that happens, we'll start our new lives where we left off—spiritually and practically speaking—when we died. The work you previously did in seeking your center and finding truth is not reset at the beginning of a new life; it's retained by the samskaras.

I would like to take a moment to address a misconception that may arise. I have often seen in Western culture images of ghosts wrapped in chains. For example, in the Charles Dickens classic *A Christmas Carol*, the spirit of a dead colleague visits the principal character, Scrooge. The ghost explains that the heavy chains he wears are penance for the misdeeds of his past life. These chains are a terrible burden that this ghostly fellow must bear, and he warns that Scrooge must mend his ways or suffer similar spiritual burdens. The story progresses from there, but we have no need to follow it further.

This notion of ghosts in chains has become so embedded in the popular imagination in the West that I doubt many people even stop to wonder why it is that at Halloween time there are so many images of ghosts rattling chains; it was one popular English author's way to describe a burden from this life following one into the afterlife. The point I wish to make is only that this is not a fitting way to think about samskaras. They are not penance or a form of punishment. A samskara is an asset of a sort, and one that will influence your next life once this one has run its course.

One may now wonder how such a seed of an experience might be transferred from one life to another, but upon consideration, it is not so strange a thought. If a man learns to drive a car, he has formed impressions, memories, and understanding of the vehicle's systems and operation. These assets all remain with the man when he exits the car in which he first developed them; they don't perish when he leaves the vehicle. You would think it odd if I suggested otherwise, because you know this to be true.

If the man enters another car, some circumstances will be different: the controls may vary from the previous car, the power of the engine may be greater, and so forth. But his prior knowledge will help him learn quickly. Each time the man started up a hill with the manual transmission in the old car—a difficult task for any new driver—informed his ability to learn the clutch in this new car. Every time he found himself hydroplaning or skidding in foul weather in the other car helped teach him how to handle similar situations in the new vehicle. I trust I don't need to belabor the point. The knowledge he gained in his previous experience will help him in his next experience, and the learning curve will be dramatically reduced. So it is with many of the samskaras carried over from one's other lives.

How is a samskara transferred when the physical body that earned it has perished? In the car metaphor, it was the physical body that moved from car to car, but in this case, it is an astral body. Muscle memory—the facility developed when we train our bodies to perform a given task until our fingers do the task automatically—is carried within the physical body. Samskaras are carried by the astral body, and not lost.

It is nearer to the truth to say that rather than dissipating or being lost, samskaras are deposited into an account of sorts. This account is not so different from a bank account. At times, deposits are made, and at other times, we must make withdrawals. So it is with the bank of samskara. Any samskara formed during a life in a physical body is deposited into this account and held for safekeeping for later withdrawal.

In this bank where we store our samskaras, there are no fees or mechanisms to diminish our holdings. There are no fees or charges of any kind—as opposed to modern banking, which seems like a game set up so that if you give the banks money, you must struggle with them to keep it. They charge fees for many services, all while making money for themselves by investing the money you have provided. In this sort of bank, we always want to see our accounts grow ever larger, as difficult as that can be, and we would be driven to deep unease if the account grew smaller. The opposite is perhaps true of the bank of samskara.

We work for an unknown number of lifetimes—because this varies from person to person—on this journey of ours from life to life, depositing samskaras and withdrawing them for use. Unlike with a bank that holds our money, we are better off, in a sense, when we see our account dwindling. This means that we are using up our assets, making good decisions, and not forming many new samskaras. Eventually we will exhaust our account of its samskaras, and then our journey will have come full circle.

To understand samskaras, let's look at a fairly ordinary journey one might take. John Doe plans a short business trip from his home in Arlington, Virginia, to Boston, Massachusetts. He gathers everything he needs for his presentation and packs his bags. After saying goodbye to his wife and children, John hops in the car and gets going. He takes his computer, his cell phone, and other such tangible items, but that is not all. We know his family is staying behind, but what—other than his bags—will be coming with him? He also brings his knowledge, his intellect, and all his plans for the presentation and for the future of his company. He brings numerous karma chains, his hopes and fears, and the feelings attached to each of them. It is likely that he brings with him more intangible things than tangible, though he may be unaware of this.

Let's say that John's drive to Boston is pleasantly uneventful. His presentation is both flawless and well received. He makes the business deal of his life, and he calls home with the news. Each member of John's family takes a turn congratulating him and expressing their love. They can't wait to see John again and celebrate this landmark moment in his career.

John places his bags into the car again, and along with his newly bolstered hopes and dreams, he heads south, back to Virginia. Traffic is light, and he makes good progress. He smiles even as he pays the toll and enters the highway, planning the future of his company. That future looks brighter than ever after this deal. With a bang, a car ahead of him gets a flat tire and swerves suddenly into his lane. John has no time to avoid it, and the collision is terrible. A five-car pileup results, and John is pulled out of his car by paramedics. By the time he reaches the nearby hospital, it is too late for him, and he is declared dead.

John's death occurred so suddenly, and on the cusp of such good things coming into his life. His family, friends, and business partners all mourn his passing, because in their eyes, his story is over. But is that truly the end of John Doe, or is he still around in some form, perhaps in another dimension invisible to us?

We, as modern people, are aware of various energies—such as radio waves and various forms of radiation—that surround us every day, but that we cannot detect with our senses. Other things that we can register with one sense but not others are swirling about us as well. We cannot see fragrance, taste sound, or feel color, but we sense them all the same. We will come back to this line of thinking in the final chapter of this book, but for now, let's presume John's physical body is of no further use to him.

John's astral body exists independently of his physical body, and leaves that broken body there in the hospital morgue. John's car is being hitched to a tow truck; the car and his bags have to stay behind as well, as John's astral body departs. However, John's astral body does not leave empty-handed. It takes along with it John's karma chains, his emotions, his attachments, his plans for the future . . . all of these intangible items that we call samskaras. His astral body then sets out on a journey to find another suitable birth, so that he may carry on, preferably at a point of progress near where he left off.

You see, samskaras are the primary driving force behind rebirth into another physical body. When a life comes to an end, and the physical body dies, the samskaras from that life act to force a new birth to occur. In this way, we start out in our new lives and new bodies in the same place we left off when we died, spiritually speaking. The work we have done seeking our center and finding truth is not "reset" at the beginning of a new life; it is retained because of these samskaras in the virtual account.

But when the being who had been John Doe takes another birth, what happens to the memories and other intangible items that came with him from that life? Why does he not remember anything? To put it bluntly, why do *we* not remember anything from our past lives?

Death and rebirth are part of a system created for the spiritual infrastructure that we talked about in the first chapter. Perhaps that seems wrong to us. Maybe we can do better. Let's consider what you and I might do if we were to reimagine the system. Suppose we decide to do away with death. Nobody likes death; it's terribly sad, and it seems wasteful, don't you think? All of this effort, all the striving and building something for ourselves, and—bam! We die, just like poor John. No, thank you. Death is off the table.

Any system needs to be internally consistent, so death-lessness has to be for all animals, plants, and naturally, all humans. Can our planet support that? Clearly, it cannot. If we rolled out a system with no death tonight, we would all be starving by morning. We wouldn't die, of course, because we outlawed it. But, we would see very soon that this new system is unworkable. A linear life, stretching out infinitely, is unsustainable. That's why this circular system of life and death has been placed in our infrastructure.

A natural question is, what happens to our memories, and why can't we remember anything from our past lives? They can be available to us under the proper circumstances. It would not serve us to have ready access to those memories simply because we're curious. Our system reveals to us what we need to see when we are ready to see it. For now, it's good we don't remember what we did in our past; it gives us a fresh start in the maya loka. But sometimes hints of those memories appear, like when you meet someone and feel instantly attracted to them or when you sense that you have known someone for a long time. It's probable that you were close to that person in your past life and perhaps will be again.

While in almost every case memories are cleansed from us for our new start at life, it's not always true. Consider Krishna; he told Arjun he chose to be born again to make himself manifest because dharma had to be preserved. Enlightened souls can do such things. Even the enlightened ones, once incarnate here, have the same limitations as the rest of us. However, they are aware of other lives they've been through. Because they exited life with full awareness and presence, they reenter life with awareness as well. Most of us become unconscious prior to exiting, and then again prior to rebirth into the maya loka.

More than anything, most of us would be confused, bothered, or distracted by our past memories rather than served by them when we embark on a new life. We are not enlightened enough to handle them, so wiping out the memories serves a practical purpose for beings in our situation.

To many people Hinduism and Indian spirituality seem synonymous with the pursuit and attainment of enlightenment. But that's true for all of us; we're all in search of enlightenment whether we know it or not. We each have an innate desire to get out of this cycle of birth and rebirth. For most, this is a result of achieving a zero balance of samskaras. At that point, we need not be reborn.

Few of us remove ourselves from the cycle through enlightenment. Don't let that shock or worry you. Enlightenment is a very hard journey, and even for very exceptional people it tends to take many lifetimes. Only one man, as far as we know, Milarepa, a Tibetan Siddha, has ever achieved enlightenment over the course of a single material incarnation. His story is fascinating, beginning with a tragedy in his youth that prompted his mother to send him away to learn sorcery. After mastering dark magic, he took vengeance on those who had wronged his family. But, regretting the lives he had taken, he later sought a holier path. After many years of wise tutelage and hard work, he achieved total enlightenment and no longer needed to be reborn.

It is much more common for an astral body to exit the physical body and find itself someplace totally unknown and unfamiliar. Let's return now to John Doe to illustrate a more typical path. His astral body has exited the physical body and finds itself someplace entirely unknown to him. John was a careful man in life, and a planner. This sequence of events—his sudden death and his reawakening after it—did not figure into his plans. Like so many of us, he did not even know that he could have also set plans for this part of his journey. He knew of no system that he could use to aid him in this most unexpected adventure. What should he do and where should he go now?

In Gita, Krishna speaks of the *varna* system. Varna was created in ancient times to make easier the journey of people like you, me, and John. It is our great misfortune that due to the broken links in our traditions, varna has been badly abused. The varna system classified people into four categories: *Brahmins,* who were the intellectuals, professors, doctors, and engineers; *Kshatriyas,* who served as rulers, warriors, and soldiers; *Vaishyas,* who made up the business class; and *Shudras,* who acted as the service class and were responsible for manufacturing, farming, and the like.

In the life he just departed, John Doe was a businessman. With varna intact, John would have had a clear pathway laid out for him. In this way, his astral body could choose his rebirth into a business-class family. This would smooth his transition from life to life and his ongoing contributions to the business community. John may still come back in the right country and to an appropriate family, but this would be easier and more assured if the varna system were uncompromised and in a healthy state.

Modern interpretations of varna as a rigid caste system are not criticisms of true varna at all. I must nevertheless point out that these negative views of varna are a fairly recent phenomenon, and based on modern, corrupted versions of the system. When it was established, in antiquity, varna was put in place to serve us all. This was accomplished by guiding each of us into a new life that would best allow us to pick up where we left off, given the samskaras we brought with us at the time of our death. Think, perhaps, of video games that allow you to restart at the same level when you die, retaining whatever in-game assets you had at that unfortunate moment. This is a far more benevolent system than one that unhelpfully assigns you to a random part of the game, or worse—makes you start over from the very beginning with empty hands.

The notion of a samskara being both an asset and something that prompts rebirth might be confusing to some. This would necessitate conceiving of rebirth as a negative, however. Certainly, some regard this cycle of birth and death as a negative thing, but I have tried to show that it is anything but that. As we discussed earlier, it is probably the best system possible. Any other conceivable system would probably be more chaotic and far less productive. Yes, it is easy to see that there is pain in this world, and it is also easy to understand that it is generally good and healthy to move away from pain. Thus, many people speak of being released from the cycle as being released from a prison sentence.

In Gita, Krishna tells Arjun that the war would happen, and that he would be dragged into it, whether soberly or with great rage after the first of his brothers was killed. His involvement was not in question—it was not really up to him—but how he'd acquit himself would be his decision. So it is with all of us as we navigate our lives.

Imagine that a drop of rain falls onto a mountain. It strikes the stone, rolls down onto the soil, and then soaks through to join an underground stream rushing through the darkness. In time, it emerges on the surface in a stream that, by and by, joins a river and winds through many miles to become one with the sea again. The raindrop may complain about the harshness of the stone, resent the soil for dirtying it, hate the darkness, dislike the course of the riverbed. But what use would there be in it? What purpose would it serve to dread evaporation into the clouds and the transition to rain once more? Ultimately, it will make the journey all the same. There is no other course for it; this is the cycle and the nature of water. Just so, there is no other course for us but the one we are on.

Life is occurring and will continue to occur. There will be unpleasant or even terrible things that happen along the way. Live a good life and have faith, and you will be taken care of by the unseen hand of grace. Some misfortune will still befall you; this is simply part of life. Pain is only a passing experience, a feature of the illusion, and thus is only a part of the great journey. The only reasonable response to life is to find the joy in it. Accept it for what it is and strive for personal growth and success.

Let us take the example of Krishna himself. His birth was not necessitated by samskaras that he still needed to bring full cycle, because he had a zero balance there. He *chose* to be born. And, as we have spoken of, he chose to be born because he knew he had a job to do: he needed to preserve dharma. Some might consider this a grim task. Krishna came to the maya loka and took a physical body in order to struggle against tyranny, oppression, and lawless cruelty. And, what did he do with so much of his time? He played the flute. He laughed. He rejoiced at the wonder that is life on Earth. Who among us has a more serious and high-stakes path set out before us? And yet *we* frown and worry, while *he* laughed and made music. Forgive me if I suggest that his way was far better than yours and mine, and we would be wise to emulate him.

Krishna was free from useless worry and unhappiness, but not because he was unaware of how harsh life can be. It was not because he was blind to suffering or to injustice;

combatting those things is the very reason he caused himself to be born! No, Krishna was able to be happy because he stood in a higher place and he saw the whole picture. Let me offer an example of his perspective on that most alarming aspect of human life—death. Krishna speaks of the cycle of lives in this way: "As the embodied soul continually passes, in this body, from boyhood to youth, and then to old age, the soul similarly passes into another body at death. A sober person is not bewildered by such a change." (Gita 2:13)

"A sober person," in this case, can be understood to mean one with a clear mind. Certainly, an anxious person can become upset that they are leaving youth and maturing into adulthood or leaving middle age and entering their "golden years," as I have heard them called. But most of us, I think, accept these very gradual changes with some grace. So it should be when a person considers that this life will soon end, and then a new one will begin. It seems daunting, I suppose, to a person who is uncertain that this is what will happen, but in my mind, that is only a person who is not in possession of the truths I am working to share with you.

You and I have been born. Surely, this means we have work to do and parts to play. I have heard it said that, if life is a drama, we should play our parts brilliantly and to the fullest. I think this is true. Surely this cycle of life is a series of blessings and opportunities, whatever our social status or situation in life. We were born, and born human. The very fact of our humanity gives us great opportunities for growth and progress on our journey from life to life.

Consider a bird. A bird is born with certain innate programming, commonly called *instinct*. It plays out its instinct, learning to fly, finding food, building a nest, and so on. While I cannot imagine it is a negative thing to be born a bird, this programming represents all a bird will do in its lifetime. It will not make progress as a human can make progress, through contemplation and cultivation of a higher state of being. It simply has no capacity for spiritual endeavors that we know of. Neither is a bird capable of bettering its world. It will leave no legacy. Its offspring will live the same life as it did. Birds and other animals bring no lasting improvements into the world and make no material progress. These are uniquely human potentials—part of our dual purpose for life in maya loka—and should be embraced.

Humans are born with innate programming, like birds or any other animals, but also with samskaras. We have the ability to create new samskaras and the ability to reduce their number, or "burn them off," if you like. In time, we may reach enlightenment through our spiritual pursuits. More likely, we will exhaust our account of samskaras and reach a point in our journey where we may choose what happens next.

There are certain card games here in the West—rummy is one example—in which one must draw a card and discard another at each turn. Each of these cards is an asset to the player. They enable the player to score points and so forth. The game ends when a player discards his last card and is left empty-handed. This, I think, is similar to the samskaras held in one's account. Each samskara, like each card in the game, has a value to it, but also weight or consequence. The end of the game occurs when the final card is out of a player's hand, and this surely pleases the winner. However, having cards or having no cards in one's hand is only a feature of the game, and not truly the point of it.

This is not unlike the management of our samskaras. Ultimately, we will move beyond the necessity of being reborn when we exhaust our samskara account. We enter a new life because our samskaras require that we continue to work until all of them are gone. We do this not because we are being tortured somehow for imperfections—atma is already perfect and always has been—but simply because it's necessary work and a part of our cycle.

We entered our initial incarnation and took our first physical body because it's in the nature of atma to explore itself. It does this through our work in maya loka. In doing this work, we tend to accumulate samskaras. In time, when all the work is done, and all the samskaras are laid down, the journey from life to life will end. It seems self-evident that you and I are not there yet; we have parts yet to play and work yet to be done. Let us do this work joyfully.

If you are an astute student of life, you will know that it's not only one's own samskaras that influence our early lives. The desires of one's parents play a significant role in our development from birth. Our parents govern financial concerns, educational opportunities, and many other factors in our lives. If one needs to be reborn, and one's parents play a large part in what sort of life we'll be living in our new physical body, is there a way to choose parents who might be better at getting us where we need to go in our lives?

Knowledge is power. Learning about karma chains/samskaras should not be merely theoretical. It has to be practical, and it should have applications in our lives. Here are some valuable questions for us to consider as we continue our journey from life to life:

Can I perform karma without accumulating further samskaras?

Can I plan for the next life while in this one, knowing I am not enlightened or even close to it right now?

Can I set myself up to be more prosperous in my next life?

These inquiries resemble a wish list of desires. I assure you that these are all attainable things, but not before considering desire itself. Desires in various forms provide a powerful driving force for most of our actions. Any person who wishes to live consciously and ensure a good journey from life to life must understand these desires, their importance, their power, and their pitfalls.

CHAPTER 9

An Important
Driving Force — Desire

I T WOULD BE DIFFICULT TO overstate the role of desire in our lives here in maya loka. It is said that no one gets to parmatma without going through maya loka, and we cannot do that without a physical body, because in addition to carrying the samskaras, the astral body also transports the mind and desires, called *vaasanas*. When we are between births, desire remains intact within our astral body and helps drive us to be born again.

Even without access to the senses, we yearn for sensory pleasures. We desire to taste a delicious meal and to smell the aroma of a steaming cup of tea. We long to watch the play of sunlight on water, and we ache for the embrace of a lover. But to indulge in any of these desires, we need a new physical body.

Let's continue with John Doe's journey from where we left him in the previous chapter. His astral body has left his physical body behind and taken his samskaras with him. John is now in a world invisible to our senses, casting about for where to go. His desires, as I mentioned above, are still with him, including all the plans he had for his future, and all he still wants to achieve. He somehow finds an avenue to come back to the maya loka. Reborn as a baby boy, he carries his full complement of samskaras into his new life, but he sheds the memories of the last one. He is given the name John Day, and he has a totally new start, with all the vigor, curiosity, and wonderment of youth.

Our physical bodies have sensory organs, which in Sanskrit are called *indriyas*. Each of our indriyas plays an important and powerful role in our lives. But there is also a potential for danger; any given indriya can be insatiable and is capable of hijacking our whole being if we give it enough power and attention and don't exert self-control. Our senses are never satisfied for long. There will always be another demand. Ultimately, you either take control of the indriyas and become their master, or they will control you all your life.

Indriyas make these demands through *mun*. There's no exact translation in English, but the Sanskrit dictionary describes it as an impulse. I call it *the wishing mind*. Indriyas are part of every physical body. In Gita, Krishna describes two other entities that come with the physical form: *buddhi* (intellect) and *ahankar* (identity or ego).

Mun and indriyas together form the vaasana. Mun is part of both the physical and astral bodies, while indriyas are only present in the physical body. While in astral form, mun continues to desire, but cannot get fulfillment because there are no indriyas. So we're born with a host of pent-up demands carried by our wishing mind. These are present within us as soon as we take another birth. The mun–indriyas–vaasanas complex—or mind–senses–desires complex—is a strong driving force, and there's an urgency to grow up and fulfill these demands.

The indriyas are the tools our bodies use to explore our world—sight, hearing, touch, taste, and smell—and they deliver information to the mun. Is the food savory or sweet? Is the blanket soft or coarse? Is the stove hot or cool? Mun will take this information and process it, providing the situational understanding necessary for the mind to answer the question, *Is this a thing to move toward or away from?*

Vaasana, or desires, can be expressed in positive or negative ways as a response to the above question; you either want something or you don't. This may be misunderstood as desire or lack of desire. But aversion is simply a form of desire expressed negatively. Taken together, the entire mind–senses–desires complex is the source of most of our day-to-day actions, as well as a great deal of our sense of self. Most of what we think of as "I" is this complex at work, and it is expressed in our language. *I want . . . I don't like . . .* In the best of times, this complex is the system that keeps us warm, dry, and fed. However, this complex has its limitations and is not a perfect system.

At times, the senses can take control of a person to their detriment. Consider what happens with drug abuse. An addict or alcoholic sacrifices everything else in their life to sate that one desire, to give his senses the feeling that comes from the drug. Health falls by the wayside. Personal safety is shrugged off in favor of the sensation. The love of family and esteem of colleagues, once so important to him, are no longer considerations because he has become enslaved by physical need. Only stimulating his indriya matters. The addict's journey spirals out of control, hijacked. Put another way, one indriya has taken control of his entire being.

With most desires there is often a connection to the material body if we look for it. You might trace a desire for social status, for example, back to improving well-being. But it's important to understand that desire isn't necessarily a negative thing; it's often for something healthful. Desire for safety, proper nutrition, and sanitary living conditions, to name a few, are all perfectly respectable and help a person desiring them to gain a firm footing in life. Attaining a good platform can help one more effectively practice his or her swadharma (calling and duty) in this life. Surely, no one can object to that.

Throughout history, across the world, what people do in life is mostly motivated by desire—from ordinary endeavors, such as pursuing a career and starting a family, to extraordinary feats. Albert Einstein was not seeking enlightenment and a deepened connection with the Divine when he researched and developed his theories on the space–time continuum. He wanted to understand the mysteries of our world, and as he followed his desire, he made discoveries and predictions we're still studying today.

A number of worthy and honorable things can and have come from following our desires. Most gurus will only warn you against the perils of desire, as if desires were always bad. They rarely acknowledge how pivotal desires are in our lives, and how often they are beneficial to us. I would like you to keep in mind that desire is not in itself positive nor negative.

One might desire one specific thing and it is good or bad depending on what else comes with the initial desire. Take, for instance, running for high office. I could run for the presidency of the United States to unite this nation, which has become increasingly more divided and partisan, with neither side trusting the motivations of the other. That wish of mine would be a positive endeavor and would echo the desires of Abraham Lincoln and poet Walt Whitman around the years of the American Civil War.

Or I could desire to become president in order to form lucrative connections that would make me wealthier than I ever could have dreamed, bring me all sorts of admiration from women, and secure my place in the history books. In other words, I could desire to hold the same public office for entirely selfish reasons, making my attempt to become president a negative thing. The desire is not the problem; what matters is the motivation behind it.

When even one desire from a single one of our senses takes complete control of a being, there is no end of trouble. A desire for safety can turn a person into a recluse or an agoraphobe.

A desire to be loved might lead to rampant promiscuity, which, in turn, could lead to being considered unfit to be loved. Desire to have enough wealth might lead one to extreme frugality and wealth hoarding. The desire for political power may lead to tyranny.

In all of the above cases, reason is put into service of mun. Instead of warning the person about the excesses in pursuing the object, reason was rendered ineffective because it was in service to the desire. The opiate addict uses all his reason to find ways to keep using the drug. The politician uses all his reason to scheme new ways to acquire power. Such is the case in these circumstances.

It is important to determine who the master will be in our human existence. If the indriyas and mun have the control, buddhi or intellect serves their needs and demands. If the control is in the hands of the individual, if *I* make decisions with discipline, my indriyas cooperate and comply.

In Gita, Krishna tells us that desire can make us drunk. It can hypnotize us and cause us to forget all else. This goes for common and great men alike. Consider Tulsidas, the author of the epic poem *Ramcharitmanas*, a book found in almost every Indian home. Today Tulsidas is widely praised as one of India's most influential figures, yet how he became a spiritual icon is instructive. As with most stories, it begins with desire. To put it gently, Tulsidas simply could not leave his wife alone. He was so filled with sexual desire for her that he could not be apart from her for even a short time. So he was beside himself when she went to visit her father. Even though she had only been gone a few days, he refused to wait for her to come home, and set out for his father-in-law's house.

This was in the flood season, and the fast-running river flowing between them was dangerous. He searched around in the darkness of night and found a foul-smelling, rotten log. He climbed onto the log, pushed it into the swollen river, and clung to it as the log floated across the river. He reached his father-in-law's house very late at night, so he did not dare knock on the front door. Prowling around to the back of the house, he discovered a rope hanging down from the upper story and climbed it to gain entry to the house. He knew where his wife would be sleeping, and gently knocked on her bedroom door. She opened the door, holding a lantern, and recoiled in shock and disbelief.

To satisfy his carnal desire, Tulsidas had not only crept out in the dark of the night; he had not only crossed the treacherous river at great risk to his own life. By the lantern's light, it also became apparent that the "rope" he had used was actually a snake. Tulsidas stood dripping wet in the doorway, shocked by the discovery, and came to another realization as the stench of death rose up from his clothes. He had not used a log to cross the river, as he had thought; he had been straddling a corpse. Moral of the story: such is the power of desire to blind a man, even one who would later become regarded as one of Hinduism's greatest saints.

While Tulsidas was driven by his baser urges, the young man who would be Buddha felt the pull of a higher passion; he yearned to understand the great spiritual mysteries. In most cases, that would be applauded, but Buddha's upbringing was most unusual. It was prophesized that Buddha would either be a great king or a great sage; the latter possibility meant he would leave the kingdom and become an ascetic. Naturally, his king father wanted Buddha to rule after him, not renounce the throne to go become a hermit.

Buddha's father went to extremes to keep his son shielded from pain, disease, and death. The king allowed only youthful people within the palace, and even hid his own signs of aging—with hair dyes and by other means—all to maintain Buddha's childlike innocence, prevent him from ever wanting anything that was not immediately given to him, and keep him at home, where he would inherit their small kingdom.

Given the bizarre schemes of his father, Buddha would never have been allowed to leave the palace had he not sneaked away, abandoning his family. Cutting off ties with his home was the only way to gain the freedom he needed to follow his desire for spiritual growth. We know now that was his true path, his swadharma. Buddha's departure from his family, which must have been unbearably painful, should be seen as a great sacrifice rather than something casually entered into.

In these stories both Tulsidas and Buddha are seen creeping along toward the thing they desired, but their mind-sets could not have been more different. Buddha's actions were deliberate, considered, and with the full understanding of their implications for his life and the lives of others, while Tulsidas was clearly drunk with his desire, unable to use his reason for anything but blindly fumbling toward his goal. But there is a commonality in these two stories that merits attention: a trigger to greatness.

When Tulsidas, smelling of rot, stood dripping in front of his wife, she held up the lantern and remarked, "If you only showed half the passion and love for Lord Rama that you show for my body, you would be a different man."

That was the trigger. Tulsidas left his father-in-law's house with new focus and determination. He found a better path, a better desire, and became great indeed. Note that the moment that changed the trajectory of his entire life occurred at the peak of his passion. We can all lose our way, even the greatest of us, but we can all find our way back as well. This is a great secret of success.

Buddha's trigger was seeing three things his father had always taken pains to hide from him. Buddha was living a life of luxury when, one day, he slipped away for a short trip outside his father's palace and saw one sick person, one very aged person, and one human corpse. That experience—no more than a random sampling of the human condition—prompted his search for the answers that turned him into the enlightened Buddha we know today.

The reactions you and I may have to any given triggering incidents will vary. Our samskaras from past lives may not be lined up yet to send us marching toward greatness. Buddha and Tulsidas were clearly almost there in their past lives. All it took was one little jolt to shake them out of their ordinary lives and onto their respective paths.

I cannot advise that you concern yourself too much with thoughts of where you may be on your own path and how far you have to go until you might achieve greatness, enlightenment, or something else. While it would be interesting to know, it would not change the work you need to do today. That is still the same, and it's right in front of you with very little mystery attached. Wishing to become great is perfectly understandable, perhaps even admirable. However, you cannot defer happiness or peace of mind to the future. If happiness is reserved for later when you are wiser or more accomplished, it will always remain there.

Desire can indeed be a problematic tool. Too little, and we run the risk of apathy. Too much, and we become immobilized by indecision. People who have the most desire tend to be the ones who take the least action. They will worry all day or daydream all day, plan and replan, and go to bed without having accomplished a single goal. They find themselves unfulfilled and unhappy. Then they rail against God because they think their lives should somehow be different without any effort on their own part. Even though the responsibility for their circumstances rests squarely on their own shoulders, they don't see it. Perhaps they don't wish to because that would mean they'd have to stop planning and imagining, and actually *do something*.

Before we get too carried away in considering the hazards of desire, let me again point out that desire is important in our lives. Would we achieve scholastically if we did not want to secure a good career? Would you have picked up this book if you did not desire to learn? Desire is a useful and worthy tool. It simply bears watching, so that our desires serve us, rather than us serving them.

At the beginning of Gita, Arjun's desires ruled him, and all his intellect was focused on avoiding his duty. They were not unworthy desires; he wanted his family and loved ones to be spared the ravages of war. He wanted Duryodhan's evil to be stopped, but did not want to pay the price. All of these desires left Arjun divided. He was of two minds, as they say in the West. This divided state is always the way when intellect serves desire.

The mun–indriyas–vaasanas complex is part of the infrastructure that drives our journey from life to life. After the deaths of our physical bodies, when we leave behind our indriyas, our astral bodies have a mun–vaasanas complex that keeps the wants going. Then we are back to seeking birth again to satisfy these wants.

It's often said that enlightened ones are not guided by their desires, so what drives someone like Krishna, Ram, or Buddha once they are enlightened? If we abandon desire, we do not become immobile and apathetic. When desire stops the intrinsic force, the driving impetus from atma, is free to flow. That force is stronger than desire; a person acting under its directive is capable of doing more and with better results than before. Driven by our intrinsic force, we will find ourselves not only accomplished, but also prolific.

While desire provides a useful drive—and has done much for us throughout history, like both ego and attachments— desire must be dropped to reach deeper toward the center. Then we can be both more effective in this world and closer to the Divine—which, you will find, are one and the same.

In such a state of centeredness, the intellect is squarely in service to the action, undivided, and with a singleness of purpose. Actions can then be undertaken without deep attachments forming new samskaras to carry with us. Instead of fighting itself, the whole of a person's being is driven forward to the task at hand, propelled by intrinsic force. Parmatma's grace buoys the efforts of the individual, and those unknowns that some call *luck* or *fate* begin aligning to bring about success.

CHAPTER 10

A Centered Being
Has Mental Clarity —
Sum-Bhava and Ek-Buddhi

I N GITA, KRISHNA NEVER TELLS Arjun what he must do, even when Arjun begs him to do so. Instead, Krishna works to bring Arjun to a clear state of mind so he can understand and perform his duty. In Sanskrit, that mental clarity is called *ek-buddhi,* and is a characteristic of *sum-bhava,* or centered being.

We often speak of mun as the wishing mind, and buddhi as the intellect. But when we think of our mind, we often relate its functioning to our brain, which is not really the right relationship. I want to clarify that mun and buddhi are not part of our brains. The brain is important for learning and gathering knowledge as well as regulating various bodily functions such as breathing. But neither mun nor buddhi is part of the brain nor derived from it.

Some cultures used to think that the heart is the source of our emotions. A fair number of traditions still reflect this outmoded belief. Stylized hearts are symbols of love, and something said with deep emotion is said to be heartfelt although we know that feelings and emotion are not actually part of the heart. We also have difficulty imagining mun (the wishing mind) and buddhi (intellect) to be separate from our physical brain, although they are. The distinction is important because it will help establish what stays behind when we die and what travels on with the astral body. The anatomy of the astral body has different components than that of the physical body, including our mun, buddhi, identity, emotions, and samskaras. The astral body's components are materially indestructible. Unlike the vulnerable elements of the physical body, such as the brain, heart, and liver, no violence can harm them.

Arjun offered Krishna one of the most eloquent descriptions of mun I ever expect to see: "The mind is very restless, turbulent, strong, and obstinate, O Krishna. It appears to me that it is more difficult to control than the wind." (Gita 6:34)

Trying to bring mun to stillness is like trying to give a shape to water without using a container. But you need to control your wishing mind so that it does not control you. As Krishna said, "For those who have conquered the mind, it

152

is their friend. For those who have failed to do so, the mind works like an enemy." (Gita 6:6)

Krishna had a two-part formula for conquering the restless and formless mind: practice and nonattachment. Mun wanders, with thoughts running in every direction at once but always moving. Thoughts are in constant transit, rushing haphazardly through our minds. Krishna teaches us how we can deal with this constant traffic through meditation. But before we can even begin, our wishing minds resist being constrained.

Mun is unruly by nature, and like any wild thing, does not submit easily to taming. Where there is meditation, there is no mun, and where there is mun, there is no meditation. Mun recognizes meditation as a threat and seeks to raise barriers against it. That's when mun engages the help of buddhi, which comes to mun's defense, asking very rational questions to dissuade the attempt to meditate:

What are the supposed benefits of meditation?
How can I know whether I will achieve any of these benefits?
Is meditation part of some religion or cult practice?
Can I ever really control my mind, or am I fooling myself?

In these and other ways, our minds will attempt to poison the well, making meditation seem foolish or undesirable.

Buddhi is so very clever and will adopt a second tactic, offering different things that could be done instead of meditating. These will often be beneficial and noble things, like the following:

> *I could exercise; that would clearly be of benefit to me.*
> *I could give my career trajectory some thought, like as my father always tells me to do.*

As you see, the first step in meditation is overpowering the mind's resistance to engaging in it. Even if your mun grudgingly agrees to start meditation, it still seeks ways to procrastinate or to get out of it. Any practitioner of meditation should be aware of this and be prepared to counter it. When Buddha was in the late stages of his meditation, the demon Mara attempted to seduce him with visions of his beautiful daughters. Mun is at play in this story, just as it is in our own attempts to meditate.

The second part of Krishna's prescription for taming a wandering mind is nonattachment. While attachment and detachment need attention and energy, nonattachment consumes no energy. Krishna and Buddha both talked about this state of mind, although in different terms. Buddha used the word *vipassana,* which can be translated as *witnessing.* Krishna calls it *vairagya,* which means *nonattachment.*

As you watch your thoughts come and go, witnessing them but not imparting energy into them, they do not take root. Giving a thought energy and allowing it to attach to an indriya will enable mun to enlist buddhi and pull us out of a meditative state, driven by the newly formed desire. If we

154

provide no fertile ground for the thoughts, they will come and go, rise and fall as we merely witness them. This is where meditation starts progressing in the right direction.

Meditation can be described very simply as a technique for exploring the energy within, and it's not so much a thing we do as it is something that happens to you. Unlike inspiration, which mysteriously comes as it pleases, we can deliberately create a situation in which meditation can take place, making it more akin to sleep. When you make your bed, lie down, switch off the lights, close your eyes, and relax, you are preparing to let sleep occur. Preparing for meditation is very similar.

Krishna described getting ready for meditation to Arjun. He spoke of sitting on an *asana* (cushion) made of layered, nonconductive materials like kush grass, deerskin, and cloth because energy must be conserved. Every house or dwelling should have a spiritual or a sanctified place that's not part of day-to-day living set aside for meditating, which should be performed at the same time each day. After repeated sessions, the vibrations and energy around that time and place become especially conducive to slipping into meditation.

Once settled on the cushion, hold your body, neck, and head firmly in a straight line, an energy-conserving posture that reduces gravity's effect on the body. We need to remember: gravity pulls down, but grace goes up. Looking at the tip of the nose conserves energy going out through the eyes. Attempting

155

meditation with the eyes closed is possible, but has the potential to make us sleepy. To avoid that, try gazing at the tip of the your nose without allowing your eyes to wander. Most of our energy goes out through our eyes unless we make efforts to prevent this. Krishna also placed emphasis on celibacy because the other major cause of energy loss is sexual activity.

At its core, meditation is a practice composed of conserving energy, creating energy, and directing and dissipating energy while staying nonattached to one's thoughts. Krishna emphasizes the "practice" element of this. With sufficient practice of meditation, you and I can conquer the mun. More accurately, we do not conquer the mind, so much as bypass it. The mind stays where it is; we just go beyond it. When we accomplish this, it's the first time we realize existence without mind. There really is such a place, and that place is where sum-bhava and ek-buddhi become natural. Building upon this allows us to reach the status of sum-bhava and attain ek-buddhi, two concepts that I will explain shortly.

Please understand that I have only scratched the surface of meditation here. This book is an overview of the journey from life to life, not a primer on meditation. That would be a worthwhile book to create, but it is not today's labor.

Most humans can and do manage our great journey reasonably well without the benefit of meditative practices. Arjun, for example, mastered archery and completed various other forms of education without meditation. However, to achieve the level of success Arjun needed during the coming war, Krishna found it necessary for Arjun to know about the meditative process and what it led to becoming. I cannot say whether Arjun had time to practice meditation before the war, but this knowledge must have helped him materially.

Let us return to the battlefield conversation of Gita. Having learned about meditation and what it leads up to, Arjun began to understand what Krishna wanted for him. He was to become a centered being, or attain sum-bhava. He understood by this point what the center is, just as we do; atma is the universal center, the hub from which all of creation radiates. He learned this in the sense of darshan, or firsthand knowledge. Krishna was his instructor and was able to help Arjun understand on a deeper level. Therefore, Arjun gained a true knowledge of these principles, not only in his mind, but also throughout his entire being.

Arjun had lived his life up until this point growing his ego to its fullness and achieving great success in maya loka. All these things are on the outer hub of life, as it were, and he found himself at a loss in determining how one manages this "centeredness" his longtime friend-turned-guru spoke of. It was clear to him that Krishna wanted him to become a centered being so that the right actions would flow from him like water from a spring, but what does that mean? Arjun began to ask questions of his friend in hopes of understanding: "How does

a centered person talk? What is his language? How does he
sit, and how does such a person walk?" (Gita 2:54)

Arjun's magnificent understanding of Divine truth is so
new and disorienting to him that the great warrior begins to
ask questions like a wide-eyed child. All the same, one might
expect Arjun to know better than to ask these things. Didn't
he fight and laugh and eat and drink alongside him without
any notion of his friend's Divine nature? No one guessed it
was because Krishna was—to them—simply Krishna, their
friend and colleague. Certainly, he was exceptional in a number
of ways, but it was not as if he were "speaking in tongues,"
as the Christians call utterance of Divine language. Nor did
he have blue skin, as he is traditionally depicted in various
art; this is an artistic convention only, which helps to set him
apart from the crowd.

No, Krishna walked like any other man, spoke as his
contemporaries did, ate the same foods, slept in a bed, played
the flute, and all the rest. He had a physical body and did the
things a physical body does. It could be no other way; when
we are here, incarnate in the maya loka, we must act the part,
and even a god is subject to this rule. Of course, there are
differences between a centered person and one who knows
only life at the perimeter, but they are subtle.

Let us imagine I am sitting at home on a winter evening.
I am perhaps drinking coffee and eating a samosa as I read

by the fire. These things are very enjoyable to me. They are products of my life, my complex of ego. The food, the drink, and the fire all delight my senses, and the reading delights my mind. I am content.

Let us say, however much I am enjoying this evening at home, that I need to go out, perhaps to the market. My buddhi, or intellect, tells me I had better take the four-wheel-drive car because it is snowing. It also tells me I must drive carefully, watching for drivers who may lose control of their cars, and be careful of icy road conditions. Additionally, I must remember to bring my wallet, or the trip will end in failure. These thoughts are likely familiar to you because they are all things that would also have occurred to you as you prepared to make such a journey.

Now let us imagine that a centered person is sitting at home on a winter evening. Perhaps he has a fire, and perhaps he does not. He is content either way. He is his own cheering fire. Perhaps he has food and drink, or perhaps not. Hungry or sated, he will be content just the same; he knows that either condition is a passing phase. He may be reading, or he may only be sitting quietly, alone with his thoughts or lack of thoughts. He is happy in his own company and needs no distraction either to soothe him or to stimulate his mind. What might we think of such a person? If he had none of the comforts we enjoy but seemed content, we might simply think him a little strange, but pleasantly so. Krishna describes this sort of person to Arjun in Gita 2:56: "Misery does not agitate his mind. Happiness is not hankered after. A man who is free from affection, fear, and anger is said to be a centered man."

Now imagine that this centered being must—like me—go out to the market on that same winter evening. He faces the same conditions I do, and just the same as for me, his intellect rises to the occasion to help him undertake the trip. He realizes that he should take the four-wheel-drive car, that he should drive extra cautiously, and that he must remember his wallet or come home empty-handed. The centered person lives in the same world as the rest of us and must employ the same tools as we all do to get anything done. The chief difference lies in his motivations to use the tools.

We are accustomed to desires spurring actions, so it is understandable to think that, without desire, we might see only inaction. This is similar to our earlier discussion of attachment versus nonattachment, and the one is very much bound up in the other. Let me give you another example of this desireless reaction to need that can prompt action.

You are hiking in the foothills near your home, simply out for a pleasurable afternoon of walking in nature. You see a stranger sitting on the side of the path. He's not looking well. You wave and call out to him, asking if he is all right. He says that he did not bring any water and has stayed out too long. You see that he is surely dehydrated, and no sooner do you have this thought than—what happens? Your hand reaches into your backpack and produces a bottle of water. You hand it to him, and he begins drinking.

We can turn the clock back and reframe this action in terms that we know. We can say, "I saw that he wasn't doing well, and I wanted him to get better," or "I just saw that he needed the water more than I did," or other such things. Certainly, these are good motivations, but they do not exactly represent what happened. You did not soberly consider whether or not he needed your bottle of water more, or whether or not you would be OK without it. You did not pause, worried that this was a trap of some sort and he meant to mug you and take your backpack. You simply saw his need, and you reached for the water at the same moment. This action was like a reflex in you. Some would say the act came "from the heart." I will say that it came from the center. This was akarma. It was pure, born of no desire, and carrying with it no attachment.

When I say "pure," you may understand that I mean not soiled by desires, but perhaps this phrasing bears examination. Soil is not bad in itself. In fact, we would be in a terrible position without soil; we need it. This is much like our desires. We need them to do much of the work we do here. It should be understood, however, that work done without desire is superior, like drinking water without sediment in it. No, having the desire is not the problem. The problem arises when the desire *has you*.

In the right hands, even a dangerous passion, such as anger—the deadliest of them all—can be a useful tool for accomplishing a worthy goal. My favorite example comes from the Ramayana epic. I have told you that Krishna was the eighth avatar of Vishnu, who preserved the dharma. The seventh of Vishnu's avatars was called Ram, and he is considered one of the most virtuous heroes in the Indian canon. He was a devoted husband, and his marriage to Sita is still discussed today in India as a model for every couple to strive for. He was also a warrior of tremendous power.

The part of his story I wish to focus on here is a brief one. His great enemy, the demon king, Ravan, kidnapped Ram's wife Sita. To reach her, Ram needed to cross the ocean. He proceeded to give blessings and offerings to the ocean god, Varun, requesting that he be allowed to cross. This had no effect. Varun did not appear nor lend any aid. Not to be deterred from the rescue, Ram took up his powerful bow and threatened to launch arrows into the ocean, which began to dry up under the perceived attack. At this point, Varun appeared and pleaded with Ram to stop. He showed Ram that among his own forces was an architect who could build a bridge across the waters. This architect was brought forth from Ram's army, and he set to work, commenting that Ram's threat had succeeded where his love had failed.

Now, it is important to note that Ram came to Varun first as a supplicant. He came with worship and love, and only when that did not produce the needed results did he employ anger. I say "employ" because it was—for Ram—a tool that he used to do a necessary job. We can understand this as tapping into the fourth pillar, efforts, for another tactic to utilize. Because Ram was centered, he took up anger just as he took up his bow, and when it was no longer needed, he released both the anger and the weapon. He did not let anger rule him or contaminate his being. He was its master, and thus he could use it and forget about it. This is no easy feat, but it is an excellent answer to Arjun's questions about how a centered man walks and talks.

A centered being can see even his own anger, affection, and any other emotion as something like a guest in his home. Thoughts and emotions come, stay for only a little while, and then they leave. One who is sum-bhava, a centered being, can observe these thoughts and emotions, examine them, and accept them for what they are—and they are most certainly asat, or impermanent. Some emotions—grief for example—can give one the impression that they will linger forever, but it is never so.

Krishna says, "A centered person is the master. He understands the separateness of sense organs and their relationship to the attractions and aversions. Knowing this, he wanders amongst different sense organs with happiness and tranquility. Such a person is content within himself." (Gita 2:64)

This awareness of self, this observation and monitoring of one's own thoughts and emotional state, is part of being a centered person. I have often heard emotions described using weather terminology, and if this is so, then the centered one has his own consistently agreeable microclimate. He will not be infected by the stormy anger or the dismal, drizzly sadness of another. In fact, he is unaffected by all external factors, maintaining always his internal clear skies in hardship or ease alike. He knows—truly *knows*—that all these things are temporary, and his eternal soul is untroubled by them.

Another key to understanding the mind of the centered being is ek-buddhi, which we may think of as *singular focus of intellect*. This state of mind is a key to both the centered being's inner peace and his outer effectiveness. If a mind is cluttered with passions and desires, it will be divided, as we have discussed. Ek-buddhi is the opposite of this, and is often described as a *single-pointed mind*, or *decisiveness*. The entirety of the intellect is working on the one point of focus. It should be understood that this occurs because the drive of such a person comes from the center—that single source—rather than from multiple origins, such as conflicting wishes and desires.

We must be careful to understand that desires will arise in a centered person. He is not without emotion or without passions; he is simply the master of these things. He sees these things for what they are—temporary, changeable, asat. Instead of believing that these passions are all that is, he knows they are impermanent and mustn't be allowed to rule him to the detriment of what is important. The wind generated by the beating of the moth's wings does not blow out the lantern. It remains steadfast in its purpose and lights up the night.

I might take a moment to point out the difference between the ease of being unaffected by the comings and goings of desire, and a more commonly seen trick, which is, controlling those passions. This is the lid pressed firmly on the pot by a person who knows intellectually that it is in his interest to refrain from being ruled by passion.

While it may seem that I am saying that centeredness and the clarity of mind that flows from it are almost superhuman, you are familiar with examples of this in your own life, though you may not have thought of them in this way. I gave you my example of acting without thought or attachment: giving water to a thirsty man. This happened to me while I was hiking into the Grand Canyon with my wife. You surely have an example of your own, if you give it some thought.

For another example of ek-buddhi, I will share something that happened recently while visiting my grandchildren. Three of them wanted to play a video game—Mario Kart—and they needed to choose their characters. The two eldest children chose quickly, with what appeared to be very little difficulty or deliberation. Then my seven-year-old granddaughter needed to choose her character. She considered and she reconsidered. She pondered this one and that one, and we all waited for her to choose so that the game might begin. After five minutes, she turned to her older sister and asked which one she should pick. There were so many choices that she could not make a decision.

We all face problems involving many options in our everyday lives, and must decide which route to take in solving them. The older children in my story had no trouble choosing because they had enough experience that it hardly seemed like a choice at all. Perhaps this character was stronger in some way than another, or that character was better at maneuvering. One might have simply been more charming. Whatever the factors were, the older children knew what was most important to them. They knew what mattered most to them, and made their selection swiftly and easily. This is a simple example of ek-buddhi.

It can be as uncomplicated as a cook in a restaurant selecting which of his knives is proper for the food he is cutting. Or, it can be the diner choosing the spoon over the fork when the pudding comes. A single-pointed mind need not be mysterious. We know it already in many simple forms. With centeredness, we know what is most important, and we can act decisively, even when the problem might at first not seem so simple.

Perhaps the closest we come to ek-buddhi or decisiveness in our daily lives is being professional in our approach. A surgeon cannot be of two minds about whether to cut a structure or not. A bomb-disposal specialist has to sever the right wire swiftly, or the results could be devastating. Arjun could not be hesitant about which arrow to use. Every split second counts. Clarity of mind is needed in all these situations because a timely decision is crucial in each. Many times, a surgeon who is indecisive about a procedure takes longer in surgery, risking greater strain on the patient. Or, he or she defers the decision altogether and seeks a second opinion. Of course, similar situations may occur in various aspects of our lives, not only the professional part.

To avoid confusion, let me clarify that ek-buddhi—or, focused decision-making—while of utmost importance, does not necessarily come from meditation alone. As with Arjun and his archery, many people attain great heights of expertise and decisiveness without meditating. Practice and nonattachment are the keys to achieving that single-pointed mind-set, but—as we have learned—meditation is a great aid for cultivating nonattachment.

Surgeons can be swiftly decisive because they have learned the procedure through training and practice, and they are not attached in any way to the patient. In fact, most surgeons would prefer not to operate on their relatives, precisely for the reason of avoiding attachments that might compromise their decision-making. A similar process happens to some extent if you assume an important platform—joining a corporate board of directors or becoming president of a country, for example. You must disclose conflicts of interest to reduce the possibility you will play favorites.

We have now spoken a fair amount about achieving ek-buddhi in practical terms. The next question that must arise is this: How can you and I achieve and maintain the centeredness Krishna encouraged in Arjun? The next step after understanding our true nature, as you have begun to do, is practicing what we will explore in our next chapters: karma yoga and results management.

CHAPTER 11

Managing Our Actions — Karma Yoga

W E HAVE NOW SPOKEN A fair amount about achieving ek-buddhi in practical terms. The next step is maintaining the same centeredness Krishna encouraged in Arjun by practicing karma yoga and results management.

You will be familiar with the word *yoga* as it pertains to stretching and strengthening exercises. Patanjali, who wrote the great treatise *Yoga Sutras*, is the father of modern-day yoga. In the book he defines yoga as *cessation of mind*. The first verse of the *Yoga Sutras* reads, "Now, the discipline of yoga." Those who take up his teachings must abide by certain rules, and Patanjali simply says that before you join his school, you must already be aware of the rules of engagement. Patanjali's commitment is to teaching the practice of yoga. Students receive a syllabus as well as routines and homework to do. Once you complete the course, you become a *yogi*, a practitioner of yoga. Krishna, who was an accomplished yogi, is also called a *yogiraj*, or master yogi. Arjun must have studied yoga during his early training with his guru Drona as well.

Krishna's teaching of yoga was different. He was less dedicated to teaching a class on cessation or management of mind to produce yogis. His efforts were more focused on addressing what comes next. His teaching was more about how a yogi talks, acts, and lives. Speaking as one practitioner to another, Krishna described how a yogi journeys from life to life. Krishna talked about how a yogi manages his life. Krishna was not teaching the ABCs of yoga; he was teaching management of the aspects of a yogi's life. When he taught Arjun karma management, he was describing how a yogi can manage his or her actions.

Life will continue rushing around us like a river, whether we try to steer clear of rocks and shallows, or passively allow events to sweep us along. To some it may seem like wisdom to be philosophical, and consider whatever bumps and bruises that come to us along the way as inevitable. They'll shrug and say that it was out of their control; they are merely victims of a harsh world. The reality is that they abdicated their control, trading it for the false comfort of fatalism.

As we make our journey through the maya loka, we must act to help ourselves. Whether we are keen to do it or would

170

prefer not to, we must do work. That's why the maya loka exists and why we are born into it. We have work to do and actions to take. Some of those actions, those karmas, will be accepting and dealing with the consequences that our prior actions—and actions in our past lives—have brought about. We know this, just as we know that some actions cause ripples—samskaras that we carry and must free ourselves from to progress along our journey—and some actions do not cause ripples.

This brings us to karma yoga, which is about managing karma to achieve the best possible outcome from our efforts.

In Gita, Krishna explains different aspects of karma, including how karmas may be managed to promote success. But you and I do not become more skillful by simply following one mode of karma yoga or another. We must learn a skill, practice it, and continually improve our abilities to stay competitive. Karma yoga is no substitute for mastery.

Arjun trained diligently and was very good at what he did. He was considered the best archer of his time and won every competition. Krishna built upon that by teaching him how to become even better. This had to occur for the Pandavas to claim victory in the war, given that Arjun had to enter into deadly combat with his guru, who'd taught him the weaponry skills he needed to use. Naturally, Arjun had never competed with his teacher, only his peers. Arjun also had to fight the undefeated Karn, who was a disciple of the great Parshuram. With Arjun's prowess at its height, the needed advantage over these powerful competitors could not be achieved by more archery lessons. Instead, Arjun needed to be nonattached to his work on the battlefield, so Krishna taught him karma yoga.

Gaining an understanding of karma yoga comes from familiarity with three things: *sakam karma, nishkam karma,* and *karma sanyas.* Let me clear up some common misconceptions about the terminology. Sakam karma has been translated as *selfish action*—and nishkam karma, as *selfless action.* Krishna tells us that nishkam karmas are superior to sakam karmas, but this does not mean that one is good, and the other, bad. Sakam and niskam only reflect an attribute of that karma.

Sakam karmas—actions performed with desires (*kamana*) attached—are the bulk of what we do in life. Preparing a meal for our children and desiring them to eat and be nourished is a sakam karma. Likewise, if I perform a ceremonial ritual, or *yagya,* for the benefit of all humankind, it's also a sakam karma because of my desire for everyone to benefit from it. Neither of the above examples is the least bit selfish or harmful to anyone. They are quite noble and beneficial, in fact.

Nishkam karmas are actions undertaken without kamana (desires). This is not the same as taking a selfless action, and, in fact, has nothing to do with self. Self does not exist in nishkam karma; it's pure karma just happening, where you or I act as a vehicle for the karma. Krishna calls this *nimitta-matram*, being just an instrument.

Nishkam karma does not leave any footprints. It does not create any ripples or waves. No karma chains result from this type of action, and it does not create any samskaras. Like a melody resonating through a flute, the instrument is unchanged and not burdened by the tune. In this way we can see that the repercussions of nishkam karmas differ from sakam karmas, which create samskaras for deposit.

That's why Krishna was not talking about good karma or bad karma, benevolent or malevolent actions. He was not discussing right and wrong when he talked about karma yoga. He was talking about whether you have any attachment and kamana. If you are doing service to the poor and downtrodden in Africa, and expect entry into Heaven in return, you are performing a sakam karma. When you just go for a walk without any expectations, this is a nishkam karma.

I must reiterate: sakam karma is not the same as selfish action and is not always bad. People perform sakam karmas most of the time, and many are for good causes. A lot of temples survive on people going there, making offerings, and asking for certain results from their karmas. Many yagyas and acts of worship are also sakam in nature.

So it may seem odd that Krishna called sakam karma less desirable. And while nishkam karma produces no samskaras, which can be seen as a positive, the basis for Krishna's pronouncement goes beyond the pursuit of a zero balance in our account of samskaras. It's rooted in an understanding of attachment, detachment, and nonattachment. We have talked before about a surgeon performing surgery. Let's return to this example and say that a patient has a large kidney tumor. This patient has seen the oncologist, has been cleared for surgery by his cardiologist, and finally comes to the operating room. Our surgeon—whom we shall call Dr. Hope—marks the area to be operated on and proceeds to perform the surgery.

Dr. Hope is not attached to the patient; this person is a stranger. He is not attached to the renal cancer either, and moves along with the surgery without any internal conflict. After a short while, the kidney with cancer is removed, and the patient recovers from anesthesia and is transferred to recovery in stable condition. Dr. Hope has performed surgery to the best of his ability. Can he predict the short- or long-term prognosis of the patient? He can cite statistics, but he cannot predict what will happen to this particular patient. The results depend on many factors, and not just on the surgery or the surgeon.

Krishna was saying the same thing to Arjun when he said, "You have a right to perform karma, but not to the results." (Gita 2:47) This is because results depend on other factors, not just Arjun's efforts, nor yours, nor mine. Just like using the previous surgeon example, the results of a surgery depend on many factors beyond the surgeon's efforts.

174

That verse from Gita has been interpreted in various ways. Some suggest Krishna's message was, *Do your karma, and forget about the results.* Some phrase this interpretation as, *Do your karma, and leave the results to God.* This is the interpretation of others, not the word of Krishna, but it is so widespread and deeply rooted, that in my earlier writings, I have expressed the same interpretation.

However, the more I delved deeper into Gita, the more I started thinking that this interpretation raises some questions. Why would Krishna advise one thing but do something else? Why would he talk about using the five pillars for success to stack the deck in your favor if what he meant was, *Do your karma and forget about the results.* Has some misunderstanding arisen?

First of all, there is no Gita verse that mentions doing karmas and not caring about the results or leaving them to God. No such passage appears in the text. This sentiment is an interpretation, and not a verse that one might quote and examine. It is not the word of Krishna then, but simply some people's understanding of the verse. Another person on a different life path may have another interpretation better suited to his own journey.

Second, it is not very practical to do (and perhaps not worth doing) a karma without knowing what it is for. A surgeon needs to know if the surgery is appropriate and what the probabilities of a successful outcome are. Knowing how to execute the surgery and performing it as though the outcome doesn't matter is not enough. Just imagine what a patient would think if you told them, "I am not sure if you need the surgery, but I will do it because it's written on your chart. I honestly can't tell you if it will help or not, but will you sign here to allow me to operate, please?"

Why has this interpretation of verse 2:47 become so entrenched in our psyche that it has become the brand and tagline for Gita itself? I don't know the exact answer, but I can offer a hypothesis.

Gita begins with the words, "Dharmakshetre Kurukshetre," the name of the battlefield, which translates to *the land of dharma and the land of karma*. And the text tells the tale of two karma yogis having a conversation. However, most of the current teachings on Gita do not come from karma yogis. Most Gita instruction and writing in recent memory has come from people who are *sanyasis,* those who have taken the path of karma sanyas.

Those on that path seek to dedicate their lives to parmatma (the Divine) and shed the usual day-to-day karmas, such as working, marrying a spouse, raising children, and so forth. By renouncing ordinary life, the sanyasis strive to deepen and strengthen their connection to the Divine. Those who undertake karma sanyas do their work and leave the result to their god. That is the hallmark of their path. It is natural for them to come to the conclusion that the meaning of verse 2:47 is that the results are not in our control, so it only makes sense to do the karma and forget about the results.

My own path led me to be a householder, husband, father, and grandfather. My path also led me to study medicine and to work as a surgeon. It seems only right, then, that my interpretation of this verse is different from that of a sanyasi. In my view, the verse informs us that karma is only one piece of what produces results. There are other factors that affect the ultimate outcome of a given karma, and we should be mindful of those other factors and take care of them as well.

If we are to achieve positive results, we must do as Krishna does, and control the first four pillars as well as we are able. Only then and not before, does the fifth pillar (the Divine, or luck) come into play. But even that may be influenced by offerings and supplication, as Krishna demonstrates, because after we have done all we personally can, we must do what can be done to bring the Divine onto our side as well.

When all that has been undertaken, we must still await uncertain results. The outcome is not entirely in our hands, and we must then accept the results, whatever they may be. The power to effect a positive outcome does leave our hands at some point, to be sure. The key difference between the common interpretation and the one I offer here is perhaps merely where one draws that line.

The outcome of a surgery depends on many factors. Some can be taken care of by the surgeon and hospital staff, and others are in the hands of the patient. A patient can live a healthy lifestyle, have regular checkups after the surgery, and pray if he believes in the Divine. Of all the factors with bearing on a full recovery, a patient may control only some of them, but he must exhaust those options to help achieve good results from surgery. For him to do less falls somewhere between laziness and suicide. The same is true of all the deeds we do. Success is not entirely in our hands, but often far more of it rests there than we seem prepared to recognize.

Back to nishkam karma. While the lack of samskaras created after nishkam karma presents a clear advantage when comparing it to sakam karma, other less obvious advantages present themselves as well. Krishna refers to those subtleties in Gita 2:40: "In this there is no waste of the unfinished attempt, nor is there production of contrary results. Even very little of this dharma protects from great fear."

To illustrate what this verse means, let's continue with the surgery example. Suppose the doctor discovers the patient is a distant uncle of his. Even though they were never close, if the patient encountered a potentially fatal complication during surgery, would that family attachment cause emotion that could cloud the surgeon's judgment? It's likely the surgeon would request to have a colleague perform the surgery because he can no longer be nonattached.

Arjun's position at the beginning of Gita is somewhat similar. He found himself called upon to fight to the death people whom he cared about, including relatives. Arjun's attachment to these people clouded his judgment to the point where he became nearly paralyzed in terms of his decision-making. Unlike the surgeon, Arjun did not have a replacement to do the job for him, so Krishna taught him to work with nonattachment.

Understand that nonattachment is not the same as detachment. Nonattachment comes from the realization that we are never truly attached. Attachment and detachment are constructs of our own thinking, fashioned in ignorance of the truth of our nature. Nonattachment is the default status of our existence. We are all interrelated but nonattached. Realizing this, we can set our attachments aside, if need be, to get on with our work.

With the surgeon, nothing changed except that we added a kamana (attachment). Every other factor is identical: the surgeon's knowledge of the procedure, the patient's condition, the environmental factors, and so forth all remain constant. The only thing that changed was the surgeon's state of mind because he contemplated his relationship with the patient. That attachment is the sole source of his problem.

Krishna teaches us to recognize that the kamana is the culprit that must be removed so it cannot hinder the results. He taught Arjun to set his attachments to the other combatants

179

aside and to let his actions on the battlefield flow through him as nishkam karmas. For the most part, Arjun did a good job, but from time to time, an attachment crept in and began to hamper his efforts. When Krishna saw the shift in Arjun's state of mind, he gently kept him on track.

One such incident occurred when Arjun was fighting on a distant part of the battlefield, where Drona had constructed a formation. Arjun's son Abhimanyu, a great warrior, fought through to the center of the formation. Normal practice dictated that the Kaurava commanders would fight the enemy one on one, but Abhimanyu was too great a threat, so several commanders attacked him in unison and killed the sixteen-year-old prodigy.

When the Pandava brothers learned the news, they were overcome with grief. Arjun, out of his attachment to his son, vowed that he would either kill Jayadrath, a Kaurava commander who had prevented other Pandavas from helping to save Abhimanyu, the next day, or else kill himself by entering a burning fire. This caused considerable trouble for Krishna, who had to perform miracles to help Arjun achieve what he had vowed to do. Thus Arjun's attachment was not allowed to become the detriment that it very nearly was. There were a number of other instances where Krishna had to steer Arjun back onto the path of nonattachment. In many ways it was much like any instructor observing a student and making minor corrections to form.

Krishna indicated that no effort of nishkam karma is wasted. Contrary to sakam karma, even a small or unfinished effort is satisfying. There is always fulfillment derived from taking this path of action, and frustration never happens because there are no obstacles in the path of a nishkam karma.

In every part of our life, we seem to find obstacles, yet Krishna says there are no obstacles in the path of nishkam karma. We can examine that statement from two angles. First, if you do not have any preconceived expectation, whatever comes to pass is acceptable. Someone going on the path of nishkam karma does not see obstacles as obstacles. It's like the flow of any river or brook; the water starts moving simply because it must. It has no map and no attachment to any given route. If it encounters a large stone, it takes a detour around the side of the stone and keeps going with no wasted time or effort. A man on the path of nishkam karma has a friendly relationship with obstacles. He accepts them as they arise, and finds a way to work around them without undue strain.

This is contrary to a man embarking on a sakam karma, who will always have an antagonistic relationship obstacles, wasting his time and energy in becoming frustrated. An obstacle only hinders one who maintains expectations of proceeding in a straight line. That's the first point Krishna was making regarding the lack of obstacles in the path of nishkam karma.

The second aspect of Krishna's statement is that someone on the path of nishkam karma actually tends to encounter fewer obstacles. It seems that the energy of the universe flows along with such a person, and is more readily available to him compared to someone on the path of sakam karma. Whether this happens because the person's mind-set is more cool and collected or because he's more in harmony with the powers of nature is difficult to say. But the Divine—or fifth pillar—does seem to rise to support efforts undertaken as nishkam karmas. Between these two dynamics, nishkam efforts are simply more effective than they would be if muddied with attachments.

Krishna asserts that nishkam karma protects us from our greatest fears—performance, success, the worry that our life has been squandered on meaningless pursuits, that our best days are behind us, and that our future is gradually fading into darkness. We internalize society's expectations. I had a patient who was fifty-plus years old and at a very low point because his wife had left him and was seeking a divorce. That did not seem to bother him as much as the fact that she was leaving him for another woman. This shattered him completely. It took a lot of time for him to recover. That was not how his life was supposed to turn out.

This, too, is the kind of fear Krishna is talking about. We have preconceived ideas about our successes or failures, and we're always afraid of not meeting those expectations. We are social by nature, and our relationships with others in our network of ego only give us more expectations to worry about:

Will my son respect me?
Will my daughter listen to me?
Will I have a long life?
Will I die alone?

We have answers that we want and expect, but we worry about facing the opposite, unpleasant outcomes. These are our day-to-day concerns, and they are debilitating. But if we remove these expectations, there is nothing to fear. If we accept life as it presents itself, we'll never have any fear; we can simply be happy instead. But even that's not so simple, because we compound our expectations. We're afraid to be happy in the face of adversity. We think, *If my wife leaves me and I'm not sad, I will be branded abnormal. I must look sad if that happens to me so I'm not shunned.* Through an interlocking series of expectations, we perpetuate an ugly spiral. Krishna wants us to break that routine. Drop the kamana (expectation), and you drop the fear as well.

When Krishna taught Arjun to work and fight with nonattachment, taking the path of nishkam karma, he understood both the value and hazards of sakam karma very well. Over the course of the war, Krishna used the strengths of various attachments to the Pandavas' advantage and the weaknesses of attachments against the formidable Kaurava army.

Arjun had studied weapons under Drona, who had taught all the Pandavas. Drona also taught all one hundred Kaurava brothers. As the war raged on, Drona took command as the general of the Kaurava side. Nobody among the Pandava army was able to get him at a disadvantage, much less kill him. Seeing that Drona could not be defeated with weapons in his hand, Krishna devised a strategy.

Drona loved his son, Ashwatthama, who was likewise fighting for the Kaurava. So Krishna used that attachment against Drona by spreading the rumor that Ashwatthama had been killed. Knowing Drona was no fool and would need to hear the lie from someone he trusted, Krishna approached the eldest Pandava brother, Yudhisthir, who was known as a righteous man. Yudhisthir refused to be part of the plan because he wouldn't lie to gain advantage. So Krishna found an elephant also named Ashwatthama, had it killed, then told Yudhisthir to inform Drona that Ashwatthama (the elephant) had been killed. Since that in and of itself was true, Yudhisthir agreed to do so.

On the battlefield, Drona was causing havoc in the Pandava camp. Krishna planted the rumor that Ashwatthama had been killed. This began as a whisper, and then became a buzz that reached Drona, who was stunned and shocked. He was not sure whether to believe that his son was dead. He sought out Yudhisthir, who told him, "Ashwatthama has been killed—not the man, but an elephant."

But that's where Krishna's trick unfolded. He let Yudhisthir say the first sentence clearly, and then drowned out the second sentence by using conch shells to create a great noise, so Drona only heard the first sentence. Drona dropped his weapons, stepped down from his chariot, and sat with his head down, grief-stricken, enabling a Pandava commander to cut off Drona's head. His attachment to his son was Drona's undoing. If Drona had been nonattached, as Arjun was learning to be, his story would have ended differently.

Drona fought with the Kauravas out of attachments to that family. He had served them for many years, and that loyalty brought him to their side during the war. It was the same for countless others who fought in that conflict. Their attachments to the Kauravas either blinded them to how a Kaurava victory would ill-serve dharma, or caused them to convince themselves otherwise. That attachment to the ruling family cost them their lives, showing once again the dangers of actions attached to kamanas. While doing karmas with the expectation of reaping their fruits is not all bad, we should remember that we do these things with unprofitable attachment to the results.

An unfortunate result of following the desire pathway is that ripples are created by those actions. A sakam karma will have an opposite and equal reaction, and that must be dealt with in days to come. The samskaras that these actions create become necessary for us to carry with us on our journey, to be burned off at a later time. This assumes that everything went according to plan and the results of our labors were favorable. Should events unfold otherwise, we run the risk of being enslaved by our desire, having our reason hijacked, and seeing more pressing problems created than a little extra deposit of samskara in our virtual bank account.

But then again, if things went well and our sakam karma gave us results similar to what we had hoped, we likely improved our lives. Whether the karma was good or ugly will determine how difficult the possible resulting samskara will be to divest, as there is a cost to everything, whether we see it immediately or not.

I mentioned the sanyasis earlier; they renounce ordinary life to deepen and strengthen their connection to the Divine. Perhaps it's more accurate to say that they seek to become more aware of the unbreakable connection that has and shall always exist even though it seems invisible to us as we function far from center, distracted by our mundane daily activities.

Certainly this is a noble undertaking, and any work done to get closer to center is worthwhile and praiseworthy. This renunciation, which is monastic in nature, is not for everyone, nor should it be. Imagine everyone on Earth taking a vow of chastity. The future of humanity would be canceled in a single generation, simply because nobody would be having babies. No new lives would mean no rebirths for souls with work left to do.

At the beginning of Gita, Arjun wonders if he could move through the world in a way that will create no ripples at all, and found himself contemplating renunciation—retiring from his role as a warrior, retiring from his role as a husband, walking away from his friends and relations, renouncing all his past achievements and connections, and becoming a spiritual hermit and severing ties with the network of ego he'd built over his lifetime. He thought that maybe that was a way out of his predicament, and talked to his friend Krishna about choosing a life of asceticism.

After all, Duryodhan had refused to give the Pandavas back their rightful lands and birthrights. Many others had claimed that same land, and they were all dead. Land comes and goes, as does good health, vast fortune, and any other thing one might wish for in life. So why not simply renounce peacefully instead of struggling against the loss of something that he'd ultimately lose anyway?

What Arjun was contemplating might seem noble at first glance, but it was only his buddhi (intellect) playing to his wishing mind. Becoming a sanyasi would have been impossible for Arjun; his personality was not made for that path. Plus, Duryodhan wanted to rule unopposed by getting rid of the Pandava brothers. If that were allowed to happen, he could expand his reign of terror. Arjun was not considering what would happen if he shirked his duty as a warrior and let Duryodhan have his way.

Karma sanyas is a noble path that many great names have traveled. Those rishis and sanyasi have made huge contributions to the infrastructure of our maya loka, including the development of the Vedas, the Upanishads, the Puranas, the yogas, and the mantras. We are all indebted to those on this path, but the path itself is not suitable for all of us because we don't all have the aptitude for karma sanyas. Our account of samskaras may someday lead us to this, but as of today, we have not been properly prepared for such an undertaking.

Krishna was aware that monastic life was not the best path for Arjun (or for most people) and reminded his friend that renouncing the world does not automatically make a person spiritual any more than simply dressing up in monk's robes would. While both might be seen as outward signifiers of a person on a spiritual journey, neither is a path in itself. Arjun's proposed inaction was actually a negative action, which meant avoiding his duty in battle wouldn't change anything for the better. So Krishna taught Arjun to take appropriate action without attachment so he could serve dharma, stand up for his family and himself, and do what he must effectively without creating a vast new weight of samskara to carry with him.

Regarding the outcome or results of our efforts, we all work toward a result, whether we do sakam karma, nishkam karma, or karma sanyas. The result cannot and should not be left to chance or to God. Seeking support from the fifth pillar—however you understand it—is important; just know that hoping and praying is not enough. It is certainly no substitute for doing our work to the best of our abilities.

I have heard it said that God helps those who help themselves. This is surely true. The Pandavas did not win their war with the Kauravas just by praying. They also did not win simply by fighting, by being on the side of dharma, or because Krishna was on their side. They won because their overall strategy was superior: they made the fullest use possible of all five pillars.

As I hope you have become aware, the practices we discuss in this book are not only useful for the betterment of your spiritual state; they are also keys to success in your life—*this* life. None of this is simply theoretical. It can be put into immediate practice, and the trajectory of your life can be permanently altered.

Perhaps better still, with an understanding of these principles, we may do the necessary work of our lives without accruing additional samskaric baggage. Then, as we burn off the old remnants of past actions, the account of samskara begins to diminish rather than swell. In time, as we deal with the residue of old actions without building up new samskaras, we move closer to a state where our rebirth is an option rather than a necessity. So we can see how karma management is an important key to bringing us closer to the ultimate stage of our journey from life to life. A second great key to unburdening ourselves is learning the management of the results of our karmas after they are complete.

CHAPTER 12

Fruits of Action
— Results Management

RESULTS ARE VERY IMPORTANT TO me. The results of a surgery I perform can mean life or death for my patient. The stakes are not so high for most other things I do in a day, but I still care about their results. If I did not care what happened, I would not make the effort. I expect that's much the same for most people.

That was the case for Krishna when he was walking the earth and doing the work he was born to do. He planned and strategized, organized and educated, devoting himself entirely to his works. He left nothing to chance and even sought to curry favor with chance itself. Clearly, Krishna cared a great deal about the outcome of his efforts.

Buddha cared too. He sought enlightenment through many paths, dropping each one in turn when it did not yield the desired result. Eventually he achieved his intended result—enlightenment—and began to teach what he had learned. That's another way of saying that Buddha shared the results he achieved with others, improving the results those seekers achieved due to their own efforts.

Gita says that we have a right to our karma, but no right to the results. I don't interpret this to mean that we should not care about results. He clearly meant for us to do our karma and get our *phal* (results), which, to me, is why he taught Arjun about the five pillars—the keys to maximizing success: to help his friend achieve favorable results.

Along with the other pillars, the fifth pillar (the Divine, or luck) may be brought to our aid, although perhaps less reliably than the others. Still, its energy is another resource to tap into, and our work is not complete if we do not seek to employ it, such as Ram worshiping Shiva prior to embarking on his war with Ravan, or when Krishna took Arjun to Ma Durga, protector of good and harmony, before the war began. Even Ram and Krishna, who possessed no small amount of power themselves, sought to curry favor with the Divine and bring that energy to work for them as they labored for results.

We ordinary folk employ many means as well. In India, China, and many other nations, a great industry has risen up around people seeking the favor of the Divine pillar. Some will read your horoscope and happily sell you remedies to counter the bad influence of one planet or another. Others will pray for you or recite various chants and hymns to eliminate obstacles from your life. To seek Divine favor for myself, I wear a ruby to please the sun, and my wife wears diamonds to please the planet Venus. This is a very common practice. Many people in India wear multiple rings on different fingers, each of them meant to please certain planets and help them solve a particular problem or achieve a specific result.

You may be aware of the Chinese zodiac and how important 2007—the Year of the Golden Pig—was. Theirs is only one of many cultures that place great significance on numerology. This practice of seeking the aid of luck or mystical forces is alive and well in the West too. I've seen endless television advertising for psychics, and newspapers print horoscopes. All over the world, people seek help from the fifth pillar to influence events in their favor and provide the best results from their endeavors.

I have a fascination for all aspects of Divine studies. I've learned enough astrology and palmistry to let me read and understand the Vedic astrology chart and the lines on the palm. Some things have become simpler in recent times with modern technologies. There are now different computer-software programs that can construct an astrological chart and make basic predictions. You simply enter the date, time of day, and place of your birth, and the computer does the work for you. I grew up in the company of several sadhus, saints, mahatmas, astrologers, tantrics, and other spiritual leaders, so it's no wonder I find the entire Divine field so fascinating.

I've seen firsthand that it's possible to acquire certain powers along the way in one's spiritual journey. Many people stop their seeking at that point. Perhaps they believe they have reached far enough, and begin sharing these powers with others. They sometimes start an institution around themselves and become both commercially and socially successful. I had a lot of interaction with a tantric *baba* called Bhootnath. I felt such deep respect for and closeness with him, and I cherish how loving he was to my wife, Lekha, and to me. He could read one's mind and look into one's past with such clarity that it astonished us both.

I once had a patient who was scheduled to undergo prostate surgery. We went over the procedure together, discussed the risks and benefits, and I answered all of his questions. He then gave me a book to read before I did his surgery: *Positive Imaging* by Norman Vincent Peale. After reading it, I understood my patient was practicing positive imaging. Every day he envisioned me performing his surgery and everything going well. When the day came, he had an excellent outcome. I can't say how much of that good result was due to his practice of positive imaging, but I respected his dedication to covering all

FRUITS OF ACTION – RESULTS MANAGEMENT

the bases and seeking aid from the fifth pillar in a way that made sense to him. Every culture in every age seems to devise a way to harness those energies to achieve a favorable result.

I have a deep interest in visiting temples and spiritual places around the world. I make it a point to meditate in each. I have an enduring fondness and respect for the Kali temple located in the Patna University complex, close to the medical college I attended in India. I have to smile when I recall how crowded this little temple was during examination times. I visited it regularly during my time at the university. I also spent time sitting on the banks of the Ganges, and from time to time, I would meditate there as well.

Most temples have an area where people and energy may come and go. However, the statue or icon is invariably in a place where the energy can be contained and preserved, and allows only minimal dissipation. I visit those temples and places to meditate and experience the vibrations and energy within them. Many such places have a set purpose; the energies within move us toward certain results.

Appealing to the Divine is a huge part of human life and striving. This has been true throughout time, across all regions of the world and all religions. So too is the practice of having sacred sites prized for their special energies. Mount Kailash is holy for Hindus and Buddhists alike. Hemkund Sahib is held as holy by the Sikhs. Muslims are able to undergo a hajj—the pilgrimage to Mecca. Christians visit famous churches around the world and often seek the aid of a saint buried there.

All of these visits to sacred sites, rites and rituals, charts, and baubles have a common goal: seeking the aid of the Divine fifth pillar to move us toward a favorable result. We do this because results matter. To preserve the dharma by securing a Pandava victory is why Krishna included the five pillars in his education of Arjun that day on the battlefield. Krishna has instructed us to do our utmost in our karmas, and then accept the results.

As an example, I offer my own plan to do well on the Patna Medical College exam, which included attending classes for five and a half years, studying textbooks, observing patient care and surgeries, going to the little Kali temple, and taking exams. The result I received was a product of all the karmas I diligently undertook.

I was working to be the very best. But while I passed the exam, I did not achieve the top score. That honor went to someone else. That was not how I wished it, but it was the result I received for my karmas, and it was too late to change it. No one can go back and make changes in the work they have already done, trying for a better result. Despite the efforts of many great heroes who fought against them, the Pandavas won the war. The Kauravas didn't get another chance, and neither do we. When all the karmas are done and the result appears—good or bad—it must be accepted. That is the most favorable choice, even if you have worked long and hard, only to receive a bad result. In Gita 4:22, Krishna makes this point strongly: "He is always content, content with whatever comes to him. He is ready to accept any event that happens around him. He is beyond the dualities of life. Such a person centered in his successes and failures is not bound by whatever his karma may be. He always remains a non-doer."

Accepting the result of our efforts is a better path forward. Failure to do so may cause frustration and a range of other emotional disturbances. Instead of wallowing in your suffering, accept the result and move on with your life. Acceptance is liberating; nonacceptance may be a trap. Some people suggest that if you accept an unfavorable result as it is, you will not strive for better. My response to that logic is, if you allow your energy to dissipate in frustrations, venting, self-doubt, etc., you'll typically lack the energy or enthusiasm to do better. Your mind, energy, and efforts will be too scattered to improve upon the poor result, even given an opportunity to do so. Accepting a result—fortunate or unfortunate—conserves your energy and empowers you to use it in your next step or endeavor. By accepting it, you do not form an attachment to the failure, and that allows you to move onward, unbound by new karma chains.

I view verse 4:22 as the key to understanding karma yoga and the importance of accepting the results: be content and go beyond the dualities of life. A person who can do this achieves sum-bhava. Neither accomplishment nor failure can affect their happiness.

Most of us live in a state of discontent. Satisfaction is elusive, and no accomplishment or acquisition seems to please us for very long. Whatever good thing comes our way, we quickly become accustomed to it, and we lose interest, much like a child with a new toy. Acceptance is not natural to us as we are. Mun does not want to accept results as they appear; it wants to be somewhere else. Verse 4:22 does not apply to us as we are today, but we can work toward it. Something inside us needs to change. We need to set meditative routines and put them to practice, as described in Chapter 10.

Then, another realization will occur about the inevitability of results that have already come to pass. As Buddha would say, you are solely responsible for whatever happens to you and around you. On the surface, that appears to be an extreme statement, but it gives you the ultimate power, and at the same time, holds you accountable. You don't have much choice about an unfavorable result since it has already happened. It's not going to change. That does not mean you cannot appeal against it or try again. But the sooner you accept what has happened, the sooner you can start afresh.

Accepting any results that come is the end of the profit-less cycle. Acceptance does not mean we stop our efforts. It does not mean we stop planning. Likewise, we must not use acceptance as an excuse to become lazy.

Krishna's path of doing nishkam karma and accepting results may appear difficult, like most worthwhile things. It may take a long period of sustained effort to reach a point where we do these things without having to remind ourselves of it first. There may be many detours and missteps along the way.

The early stages—especially—might be easier if you were to leave home and go to an ashram or spiritual retreat. In such an environment, you would almost certainly have fewer distractions, which could enable you to dedicate more time to your centering process. Yet, while you're there, you might miss out on the excitements of normal life. That is the path Arjun chose: he returned to the life he had been living. He continued to fight. Krishna stood side-by-side with Arjun during the battles, aiding and protecting him.

Many today still criticize Krishna for his involvement in the war. Although he did not use any weapons against the opposition, Krishna planned and participated, which confuses some people into believing Krishna was a warlike or destructive force. He was not. Krishna stood for freedom, and freedom comes at a cost. He simply did what needed to be done to restore the balance of dharma.

Krishna didn't always speak of peace, but he was peaceful all the time. Even if Krishna was in the middle of a raging battle, his center was always in the same place, and he was at peace within himself. His virtue may not be as obvious to us as that of some other luminaries, but we should know that there is no real difference between him and Buddha or Mahavira.

The path to effortless karma yoga and accepting results as they come can be arduous. A lot of things can happen in your life while you are on that road. It does not matter if you seek out an ashram or stay at home; events will occur anyway. You may fall in love with someone. As we walk the path of yoga, our sensitivities increase. Passions become stronger. You start feeling with senses that are not present in ordinary life. When we embark on that journey, life becomes so vibrant.

With this increase in sensitivity and mindfulness, we become aware of the baggage and karma chains we keep collecting and carrying through our ordinary lives without even noticing. Let's say a friend insults me. One day I'll return that slight, but until then, I carry it with me, waiting to throw it back at him. When I get the opportunity, I seize the moment, and return his discourtesy. I'm happy and relieved, but only for a moment. So now I'm carrying two pieces of baggage: the original insult and my reply to that insult. My friend is now walking around burdened by both his original insult and my reply. Naturally, the instant he finds an opportunity, he insults me again. Nothing is being resolved. Our baggage is only growing. In ordinary life, we unknowingly accumulate so much of this baggage that it becomes impossible to live happily. We become so accustomed to the baggage that we only realize we were carrying it when it's truly gone.

There's a story about Buddha I think illustrates this problem quite well. A man came to Buddha one day as he sat beneath a tree, and without speaking a word, the man spat in Buddha's face. Buddha's disciples shouted and gasped and rose to strike him, but Buddha quieted them and wiped the spittle from his cheek.

He earnestly asked the man, "What next? What do you want to say next?"

The man was shocked and confused. Of all the responses he might have imagined and planned for, that was something entirely different and utterly beyond the man's belief. Buddha was not afraid, angered, or hurt by the insult because he knew the man's anger wasn't really directed at him. It was some preconceived notion of Buddha that had offended the man and had caused him to lash out. The man had been told Buddha was an evil upstart, challenging the teachings of the Brahmans and threatening the very spirit of their nation.

Eventually the man slipped away in silence, and that night, he couldn't sleep. All of his conviction was gone, as was the righteous anger that had driven him to seek out Buddha, provoke him into a fight, and kill him. The man realized he had heard wrong about Buddha, and went back to see him the next day. When the sage waved aside his disciples so the man could pass, he threw himself at Buddha's feet, shaking with tears. Buddha remarked that the man had strong emotions and was only able to express himself through wordless action. Again, he asked the man, "What next?" The man asked for forgiveness.

Buddha smiled at the man and told him that was impossible, as there was nothing to forgive and no grudge to set aside. Buddha said that he was not the same man who had been spat upon, and neither was the stranger the same person who had spat. Time and life had gone on, like the waters of the Ganges River, and all of that business of yesterday was left there. He helped the man to his feet and stood near him, saying that those men of yesterday were gone, along with whatever offenses they might have committed.

"Let us forget it," he told the man. Draping his arm around him in friendship, he added, "Though I know you are a man of few words, I am very interested in what you now have to say."

Buddha was a centered person in action, a master of his passions and his karmas. His response came from his concern for and interest in another person, rather than from anger. He sees the spitting as an expression rather than an insult. Because of that fundamental difference in the source driving his actions, Buddha kept his hands clean and also served as a catalyst for positive change in the stranger. In this, we see how a centered individual can be in the world and act without causing troublesome ripples or karma chains. When the man spat at him, Buddha wiped it away. That's it. That was the end of the action and its results for Buddha. He dropped the whole incident and went on with his day. The next morning, it was a different day and a different Buddha. That's what Krishna meant about abandoning the fruits of action. He was teaching us how to reduce the burden we carry with us all the time.

Note that he was not talking about forgetting what we've learned. He wasn't talking about throwing away the books, degrees, or diplomas. Krishna was not against celebrating a success. The successes you have won and the experience you have gained will be there to help you as you work; you don't need to carry trophies, medals, or certificates in your back pocket. Krishna's concern was with the burdens we carry unnoticed: the ego, the emotions, the grudges, and so on. Those things weigh us down, and if we want to be free to be happy all the time, we need to leave them behind as we move onward.

It's not only bad things from which we need to unburden ourselves. If something's not necessary, don't carry it forward with you. After all, you can always pick up an emotion or a tool to use in a particular situation—like how Ram used anger when dealing with the ocean god—and then drop it again when it is no longer needed.

Let's say that we do our karma, abandon the baggage of the fruits, and also drop the ego and identity that went with it. We then find that what we dropped does not simply vanish. All that discarded material remains in our memories or somewhere out there in the world. To learn how to be truly free of this refuse, it's necessary to understand yagya.

The literal translation is *devotion, worship,* or *offering,* and refers to a ritual often accompanied by a mantra and traditionally performed in front of a fire. Yagya can be described as a sacrifice for noble purposes, such as in sacrificing ego, selfishness, and material attachments, and adopting rational thinking, humane compassion, and dedicated creativity for the welfare of all, not personal gain. Obviously, that provides a description, not an understanding. I cannot point to a ritual burning and have you understand yagya any more than you can point to a Christmas tree and have someone understand the meaning of Christmas and all it entails.

My sister once came to stay with us in Maine, and my family observed her fasting on various occasions and doing things the way they are done in India, which were utterly alien to my children raised in the United States. Yagya has gone out the door in most of India and may soon exist only in textbooks.

Krishna said that karma performed as yagya is not a binding. *Karma performed in surrender to parmatma* comes closest to a proper translation, yet it does not convey the full meaning. In surrender, the individual who surrenders remains. In yagya, even the individual is gone. He is not only purified, but also evaporated. That's one reason why fire is used as the purifying agent. We see a physical fire when we burn wood or gas, but there is another fire inside of us.

Every element and individual has a fire element within them. There is fire in love, and there is fire in hate. If you take the gross element and surrender it to the fire element, then a yagya is performed. Life has an energy element inherent to it. We have talked about how meditation is about exploring energy within ourselves. In a meditative state, you can feel energy circulating through you, and your chakras vibrating.

The concept of a life force is found in most ancient cultures of the world. In India, this energy is called *prana*; in China, it's called *Chi*. For Native Americans, it is the Great Spirit. In Japan, the energy is known as *ki*, and the discipline of Reiki is based on feeling and transferring this internal energy to promote healing of the physical body. It is widely understood that you can increase and develop your prana, Chi, or whatever you wish to call it, to overcome illness, become more vibrant, and enhance mental capacity.

Similarly, we can perform yagya to make use of the fire element within ourselves and the fire element of parmatma. It's natural that we want to hold on to our karma and the results. We want the credit, we want to own the results, and we wish to retain these things, which may be why they remain even after we have dropped them. But Krishna is not only asking us to let it go, he wants to see all virtual documents of accounts burned in the fire.

We know that fire is used to purify gold. But gold is still there in the end. If we knew that gold would be burned away, no one would dare put the gold into the fire. Such is our resistance to letting go. Krishna does not want any remains left behind to burden us. Overcoming this resistance is not easy, but who says a better life is easy?

That's where yagya becomes valuable. You need to get rid of these bags, so you drop them along your path. But they still carry the tags so you can pick them up again, or someone else can stumble across them. Then they become someone else's burden. Burning them in the fire of life gives us a way to get rid of these bags and their tags for good.

The fire of life burns in all of us and in parmatma, the Divine. We have to discover that fire and make use of it. Just as Arjun did in his day, we need to burn everything—the good and the bad, the beautiful and the ugly, achievements and failures, and everything else. Then, and only then, can the pure self shine.

We began our exploration of the journey from life to life with questions such as, *Why do we work? Who do we work for? What is the driving force behind it all?* Employing yagya simplifies the complicated answers we have discussed. We work because we have to work; there is no alternative. We work for parmatma; in fact, only parmatma remains. There is karma, and there is parmatma. What is burned away in the flames of yagya is the doership. There is no one to claim the result. As to the question of the driving force, it is the fire within that drives the doing.

This is not true simply because Krishna said so. Krishna said this because he knew it to be the truth. He knew that yagya is a method for attaining excellence beyond the possibilities of an individual's limitations. It leaves behind no imprints and no baggage. It's also preparation for the final part of our journey, from end of life to coming back to the beginning. You have to leave all that behind when you finally depart your current life anyway, but that life will be better lived if you divest yourself of this burden sooner rather than later.

CHAPTER 13

End of Life and
New Beginnings

IN THE PREVIOUS CHAPTERS, WE have learned many things, from entry into the maya loka infrastructure through physical birth to attaining success by doing our karmas and managing results. This brings us to the last chapter of this book—the most intriguing one for me—where we discuss when we exit the maya loka and what comes next.

Most people do not like to talk about death; it makes them uneasy. It seems easier to close our eyes to it and concentrate on the business of living than deal with our innate fear of death. There is no shame in that fear. But we must come to terms with the certainty that each of us will someday die, a moment that draws nearer with each passing day. Still, we often wish to bury our heads in the sand and wish it away.

Better by far is to consider it soberly and begin to assuage the fear that death instills in us. We ought not think of death as a great and terrible ending, but as a great challenge and adventure, a journey into unknown territories and uncharted waters. Our death is perhaps even the greatest challenge of our life, so it's worth exploring.

We can plan for death even while we are aging better and living longer. We exercise to stay healthy; we drop bad habits and switch to a healthier lifestyle, stick to nutritious food habits, and get regular medical checkups. There's increasing importance being placed on palliative and end-of-life care. Insurance companies offer special policies so we can afford nursing home care, pay for our cremation or burial in accordance with our beliefs, have a memorial service, and even purchase a headstone.

All these efforts are in service of life, whether extending our lives or making our last few days comfortable as we approach the inevitable end. We have come a long way toward making our lives easier right up until the day we take our last breath. But what happens then? Does this huge network of support and service offer us anything more after we die than a memorial gathering and a plan to take care of our body? We might get a little plaque or grave marker. Truly remarkable people are celebrated with the likes of the Lincoln Memorial in the United States or the Taj Mahal in India. This is all quite nice, but does nothing to address what happens to our departed soul. Even our memorials are for the benefit of the living.

While most people on Earth believe that our journey does not stop at death, few of us do anything to plan for that time. Our life beyond life is often left to God, our priests, or pundits. The part of our journey that occurs after we die is often ignored, and many of us do not invest in planning for it. Perhaps it's because so little is widely known about that leg of our journey. Or maybe it's just hard to even begin the conversation that would prepare ourselves for it.

Much of what I am going to present in this chapter may sound speculative, but please refrain from judgment until you finish reading. Let me be clear: I don't need you to believe what I say. As Aristotle taught us, "It is the mark of an educated mind to be able to entertain a thought without accepting it." If you stay open to the ideas expressed here, you may find yourself interested in gaining more knowledge in this field. Even if you only seek understanding to disprove something you read here, I would be pleased. My hope is that we will all begin thinking about planning for the inevitable journey beyond death.

Our journey from life to life has three legs: birth to death, an in-between space beyond death, and traveling from in-between to birth. We devoted the last twelve chapters mostly to the first part of the journey. The in-between state—called the Bardo state—is described in the book *Bardo*

Thodol, which explains that there are multiple choices as to the direction one goes from here. The third stage of our journey from life to life is when decisions in the Bardo state result in seeking out and effecting another birth. From there, the cycle begins anew.

Bardo Thodol, also called *The Tibetan Book of the Dead,* is the first English-language translation of *The Great Liberation upon Hearing in the Intermediate State.* The Indian mystic Padmasambhava is traditionally credited with writing this work in the Tibetan language, intending it as an instructive book for those who have died. It's read aloud to the recently deceased to guide them to the next part of their journey. *Bardo Thodol* will be a key source of information as we explore the subject of our existence after death.

Let's examine what happened to our businessman, John Doe, as a consequence of his fateful drive from his meeting in Boston to his home in Arlington. John met with a fatal automotive accident. We know his body was taken by ambulance to the nearest hospital, where he was declared dead. We see that his family is heartbroken, the car is totaled, condolences are pouring in, a memorial service for him is being arranged, and so on. Sadness is in the air for everyone touched by his life. All of this is familiar to us; we have seen it many times before. These are occurrences in the maya loka, the land of the living. The interesting question is what is happening on the other side of John's death.

What happens to John Doe's existence? Where is the essence of John Doe? As his physical body became useless, John's astral body departed from it, as we discussed in an earlier chapter. This indestructible astral body carries the essence of John Doe, including his thoughts and feelings and, more importantly, his samskaras. The astral body is actually the third out of a total of seven bodies described in detail by Osho, and it is the body that carries on with the journey from life to life. Tibetans believe in talking to the astral body after the physical body's death.

After we die and the physical body becomes useless, our astral body departs from it. That indestructible astral body carries our essence, including thoughts and feelings and, more importantly, our samskaras. The astral body carries on with the journey from life to life. Tibetans believe in talking to the astral body after the physical body's death. *The Tibetan Book of the Dead* says, "Thy guru has set thee face to face before with the Clear Light, and now thou art about to experience it in its Reality in the Bardo state, wherein all things are like the void and cloudless sky, and the naked, spotless intellect is like unto a transparent vacuum without circumference or center. At this moment, know thou thyself, and abide in that state."

The astral is the third of seven bodies. The first body is the physical one. The second is the etheric body, which also separates from the physical body at death. It's also called the *emotions body.* Its form is like a vapor.

In his book *The Yoga Sutras*, Patanjali describes five bodies, while Osho describes seven bodies. We will focus on the first three bodies of the seven described by Osho: the physical body, the etheric body, and the astral body. The other four are the mental body, the spiritual body, the cosmic body—or the *brahma kaya*, and finally the *shunya kaya* or the *nirvana kaya*. The seven bodies are closely related to the well-known seven chakras.

The technique of knowing the deeper bodies begins by knowing the physical body from within. Then every other step opens for you. The moment you work on the first body, you have glimpses of the second. Each body has two dimensions: the outer and the inner. And just as a wall has two sides—one facing outward from the structure, and the other facing inward—each of our bodies has a boundary forming inner and outer limits. When you come to know the first body from the inside, you become aware of the second body from the outside. In that way, we may explore our inner bodies.

When the first body dies, the second remains alive for thirteen days and travels along with the astral body. Then after thirteen days, it, too, is dead. It disperses or evaporates. If you come to know the second body while the first is still alive, you can be aware of this happening.

The etheric second body can move outside of the physical body. Sometimes in meditation, this second body goes up or down, and you have a feeling that gravity has no pull over you.

You seem to have left Earth, but when you open your eyes, you are on the ground, and you know that you were there all the time. This feeling that you have risen occurs because of the second body, not the first. For the second body, there is no gravitational pull, so the moment you gain awareness of this body, you feel a certain freedom that was unknown to the physical body. At that point, you can travel outside of your physical body and come back.

The etheric body is put to work in hypnosis. The first body is not involved in hypnosis, only the second body. You can become aware of your second body from the inside—its inner workings, its internal mechanisms—just as you became aware of your physical body from the inside. The first time you try, it's difficult, but after that, you'll always be within the first *and* the second.

Once your exploration has led to you being aware of the inside of your second body, you will feel the outer reaches of the third, the astral. In exploring the astral there's no need for any exertion of will. Just the wish to be inside is enough. There's no question of totality now. If you want to go in, you can find yourself inside. The astral body is transparent, so the moment you're outside, you'll be inside, though you may not even know which is which.

As a point of interest, know that the physical, etheric, and astral body are all the same size. This remains the case through to the fifth body. The content will change, but the size will be the same up until exploring the sixth body, which is cosmic in size. The seventh body cannot be said to have a size at all, not even a cosmic size. Although Osho has described how to know about all seven bodies while we are alive and well, we will only discuss the first three bodies here. No more is necessary for understanding our journey from life to life than our physical body, etheric body, and astral body.

John Doe's etheric body and astral body are now outside his physical body. It was not his choice; this simply happened upon the death of the first body. He still has his mun, emotions, buddhi, and ego with him, carried by the astral body. All those business plans he made in Boston are still going through his mind. His family knows what has happened to his physical body, and the doctor, police, and all of his friends know he is dead. What these people do not know is that John is still around, but in another form. Mainly, this is because they do not believe in this possibility and they do not see John Doe's etheric or astral bodies.

John Doe has become part of his family. We all build our personal empire of existence. My father and mother are part of my being. This bonding is not just abstract: it is real. When John died, part of his wife, part of his son, and part of his close friends also died. That's why the pain is so deeply felt. Many people died around the world on the same day as John. Quite a few of those people died in car accidents, so even the method was the same. But, because John's friends and family didn't know them, no bonding or attachments had formed, and hence there is no question of pain or sadness regarding the passing of these strangers. But these friends and family members do know John Doe, and the bonds they formed with him cause them pain.

John, unlike his loved ones, does not know or believe that he is dead. He still feels himself to be intact, and all of his bonds and attachments are still with him. John can see and hear what's going on around him, and even tries to communicate. Though he can see his body and the things being done to it, when he tries to reenter his body, he can't. Can you imagine his frustration and disbelief at his inability to do anything about what is happening to him? *Bardo Thodol* describes techniques to close a womb door that we don't want to enter. This knowledge can give a soul more time to choose a better birthing. The book also tells us that we have forty-nine days from the day of physical death to enter a womb. If we choose to stay back by entering another loka—such as deva loka—we must make this choice within that time.

To understand our journey from life to life, we only need to know about our physical, etheric, and astral bodies. After death, our etheric and astral bodies are now outside the physical body, meaning we're still around but in another form. What makes the end of a life—whether one's own or that of a loved one—so distressing a thought is our attachments. We all build our personal empire of existence. My father and mother are part of my being. That bond is not just abstract; it's real. When we die, a part of those who love us also dies. That's why their pain is so deeply felt. But we do not know or believe we're dead. We still feel intact, and all of our bonds and attachments are still with us. We can see and hear what's going on around us, and we might try to communicate. Though we can see our body and the things being done to it, when we try to reenter it, we can't. *The Tibetan Book of the Dead* describes the frustration and disbelief experienced:

> When the consciousness-principle getteth outside [the body, it sayeth to itself], "Am I dead, or am I not dead?" It cannot determine. It seeth its relatives and connexions as it had been used to seeing them before. It even heareth the wailings. The terrifying karmic illusions have not yet dawned. Nor have the frightful apparitions or experiences caused by the Lords of Death yet come. . . .

> About this time [the deceased] can see that the share of food is being set aside, that the body is being stripped of its garments, that the place of the sleeping-rug is being swept; can hear all the weeping and wailing of his friends and relatives, and, although he can see them and can hear them calling upon him, they cannot hear him calling upon them, so he goeth away displeased.

John can continue to see what is being done in our world, the decisions being made. He might disagree with these choices, and even hear himself being misrepresented at times by people speaking about him. All his belongings, wealth, and assets are being distributed to people to whom he probably never meant to give them. And still, he can do nothing to change it. This is when he starts realizing that maybe he has died.

We'll continue to see what is being done in our world, the decisions being made, but will have no control over it. That's when we start realizing that maybe we've died, and all our belongings and assets we were so attached to were never truly ours. Nonattachment is the default state of all things around us, but it takes a step like death for many of us to realize this. The Tibetans talk to the person in the Bardo state, where we are at present, and say this about his attachments and clinging to them:

> O nobly-born, that which is called death hath now come. Thou art departing from this world, but thou art not the only one; [death] cometh to all. Do not cling, in fondness and weakness, to this life. Even though thou clingest out of weakness, thou hast not the power to remain here. Thou wilt gain nothing more than wandering in this Sangsara.

A story from the end of the Mahabharata gives us wonderful illustrations of end-of-life philosophy and truth. Many years after their war with the Kauravas, the Pandava brothers were at the end of their lives and making their ascension to Heaven. As they began this symbolic journey, Agni appeared before Arjun and asked him to return his bow to Varun. The Divine bow, named Gandiva, was Arjun's most prized possession.

Brahma, creator of the universe, made it, and both men and gods regarded it with fear. Naturally, there was great attachment, but Arjun returned the bow to the sea god, Varun, without hesitation, simply dropping it into the waters, as one would an offering.

As I see it, Arjun did not have any choice, just as we don't have a choice after death of letting go of our possessions, as nonattachment forcibly becomes a reality. This is not so different from our businessman, John Doe, watching his possessions being given away. Even his most favorite and meaningful item has to go; nothing remains ours. The naked truth is, you are eternally nonattached. Hopefully, it won't take our entire lives—and the ending of them—to fully realize this.

After thirteen days from the death of the physical body, the etheric body and seat of emotions also withers away and dies. That's why Tibetans attempt communication and read the *Bardo Thodol* aloud for fourteen days. Then the astral body continues with the journey into the place beyond life. While the first two bodies are perishable, this third body is indestructible. It can be transcended by knowing the next bodies, but cannot be destroyed. Krishna says about the astral body, "*Weapons cannot cut it, nor can fire burn it; water cannot wet it, nor can wind dry it.*" (Gita 2:23)

It's one thing to realize the existence of the etheric body and the astral body; this knowledge will help us better deal with our departure from our physical body. Some wonder if it can be useful while we are alive, or if it can be used as a means to exit the physical body at will with an intention to return. The answer is yes, but with a cautionary note. The existence only reveals what we're ready for, so if you think that knowing about the astral body will let you use it to commit suicide by simply abandoning the physical and etheric bodies, that won't work. Nature will not let that happen.

Many enlightened persons have used astral body travel to monitor, help, and guide their disciples on their paths of spiritual search. When I say that Krishna will come and help you when you are ready, I mean that Krishna in one of his bodily forms will come; the same applies to Buddha, Mahavira, and so many others. They could and often did undertake such travels when they were alive and walked on Earth. They continue to travel among us in some body form or another now that they are not with us in the physical form.

Travel outside one's physical body via the astral body is one practice. Another matter entirely—and a practice that is far less common—is entering another person's body (Parakaya Pravesha). A story about the eighth-century sage, philosopher, and theologian, Adi Shankara, contains an illustration of this practice. Shankara would travel from place to place and engage in debates with scholars he encountered. One day something out of the ordinary occurred. After winning a debate with a man named Mandan Mishra, he was challenged by the man's wife, Sarasavani, who had been acting until then as the debate moderator. Shankara welcomed her challenge, and Sarasavani began asking difficult questions regarding sex and other aspects of married life. She knew Shankara would not be able to answer because it was well known that he was celibate. However, Shankara did not accept defeat, and asked for some time to obtain the answers to these questions. The wife agreed, and the sage went away in search of knowledge.

Walking with his disciples and pondering how he might find the answers he needed, Shankara happened upon the body of a recently dead king, Amaruka. He asked his disciples to keep his own physical body safe in a nearby cave so that he could enter the body of King Amaruka. Traveling with his astral body, he entered the dead king's vacant physical body and went to the king's palace. He spent some time living as King Amaruka and learned much about sexual pleasure and family life. Soon, he returned to his own body and sought out Sarasavani and answered her questions. This story is an example of what's possible if we start looking and researching within rather than without.

* * *

Thirteen or fourteen days have passed since John Doe died in the physical form. Even if he were Tibetan, communication attempts and guidance by voice would have stopped by this time. What happens now that his etheric body has dissipated and his astral body is in Bardo is not very clear. There are choices or options at this intermediate stage, and once the choice is made, we leave Bardo. Rebirth into another physical body in maya loka is one of the options, and perhaps this is the most commonly taken.

For the sake of simplicity, let's say that John Doe could potentially go to either *deva loka* or come back to maya loka. Deva loka is another space with its own infrastructure, similar to the one we have for the maya loka, as described in our first chapter. Many good and great souls spend some time in deva loka prior to returning back to maya loka. There are options at the intermediate stage, six or seven lokas, each with complete infrastructures. Once the choice is made, we leave Bardo. Rebirth into another physical body in maya loka is probably the most common option selected.

In many religions and scriptures, there are numerous descriptions of Heaven and Hell. We know that our astral body cannot be burned, cut, or tortured. But most of us only understand that on an intellectual level, and don't truly *know* it. Because many of us fall unconscious before our death, it occurs in something like a dream state, which comes and goes, even for the astral body. People from all walks of life and all faiths have reported versions of this dream state, but the experiences vary. Some describe their time there as eternal torture and burning, but others describe enjoying life as a maharaja—a prince—in Heaven. It seems entirely possible that aspects of the dream state, rather than any reality, are what people report in these instances.

Some people resist becoming unconscious before death, either out of a desire to retain control of their journey, or simply out of curiosity. I'll share one great example of a man who tried to fully experience life right up until the last moment. Socrates, one of the fathers of Greek philosophy, was ordered put to death for the alleged crime of corrupting the youth of Athens. The method employed in state executions was to force the condemned man to drink hemlock, a poison that produced a slow and agonizing death. Socrates was a fiercely curious person, so rather than drug himself with something to ease the pain of his passing—as his disciples begged him to do—he was up and walking about after he consumed the poison. He did not want to miss what he called a once-in-a-lifetime opportunity, and called upon those present to take notes as he described what he was experiencing, right up until he lost the power to speak.

Socrates was not alone in wishing to be aware and active in the process of dying. Tibetan Buddhists beat a drum at the bedside of a dying person to help them stay awake and aware for as long as possible. Another path is the development of consciousness to such a level that one may travel into death with full awareness and possession of one's faculties. The symbolic tale of Swargarohan describes the Pandavas' journey to Heaven.

Long after the time of Gita, long after Krishna had opened Arjun's eyes to the sacred mysteries of life, Arjun and the Pandava brothers came to the end of their lives. Yudhisthir handed off his kingdom to a worthy successor, and the other brothers did likewise with their earthly responsibilities.

We know that every person, in the end, must pass the torch to another whose life's journey has many years remaining so the good works we have done can continue after our passing. This way, the infrastructure for all of our journeys may continue to be maintained and bettered. This continuation enriches us all.

The Pandavas, along with their wife, Draupadi, then set off to travel through India and the Himalayas into Heaven. As they left their home, a dog befriended them and joined them on their long journey. While crossing the Himalayas, Draupadi fell dead on the trail. Yudhisthir understood and explained to the others that her love for Arjun over the rest of her husbands was the vice that prevented her from physically completing the journey, forcing her to travel the rest of the way in spirit. The brothers accepted the explanation, understood the necessity of dropping their attachment to their beloved wife, and continued on without looking back, because what was gone was gone. Arjun had to give up the bow. Each of the Pandava brothers had to give up their attachments to Draupadi. There was no relationship there anymore, and from this point forward, there would be no looking back.

Next, Sahadev fell dead, and Yudhisthir explained that while he was highly virtuous, he was also vain and thought himself the handsomest person in the world. The brothers understood, and continued on without a backward glance. One by one, the brothers fell dead, and like Draupadi's mortal form, each body is left in the same place where it was discarded by its spiritual self. Eventually even Arjun fell dead on the mountainside, unable to make the bodily journey into Heaven because of his great pride in his archery. Only Yudhisthir and the dog continued on to Heaven. Yudhisthir understood that with his brothers passed on, the last of this life's attachments had fallen away from him.

On Mount Meru, the king of the gods, Indra, came to Yudhisthir in his chariot and offered to carry him into Heaven, but only if he were to leave the dog behind. Yudhisthir, the last remaining Pandava and the most perfectly virtuous of them all, could not abandon the dog. No amount of coaxing from Indra could make him leave the dog behind, and in the end, the dog transformed into the Dharma, Yudhisthir's own father. Dharma praised Yudhisthir's virtues and encouraged his son to enter the chariot and ride into Heaven, ending the story of the Pandavas in the Mahabharata.

The most important aspect of this story for us is that the Pandavas saw their closest loved ones die beside them, one after the other, and moved on without shedding a tear or looking back, illustrating their understanding and acceptance of the ultimate truth of nonattachment. All relationships are temporary in cosmic terms. Arjun, if and when he comes back to the maya loka, will have a different life; he will not be a carbon copy of Arjun as he was in the days of the Mahabharata.

In our Bardo state, we will see several options to return to maya loka, but it's unlikely we'll know how to make an advantageous choice or how to stop ourselves from entering one or another womb. The *Bardo Thodol* describes techniques to close a womb door that you don't want to enter. This knowledge can give a soul more time to choose a better birth. The book also tells us we have forty-nine days from our physical death to enter a womb. If we choose to stay back by entering another loka—such as deva loka—we must make this choice within that time period.

Some memories of our previous life are still with us in Bardo; the birthing process is where the memory gets wiped clean. Whether this is because of the painful delivery process or by Divine design is hard to know, but it does happen to the majority of us. We are born with a clean slate; our samskaras continue with us, but we are unaware of the details. We have come full circle on our journey from life to life, and the journey continues.

All of our attachments vanish when we die and take a new physical form. All of our memories are left behind, and we begin fresh to form a new system of ego and new relationships, and move again through the framework of our journey.

This is a blessing, as memories of past lives are likely to do more to confuse and unsettle us than help us. Imagine how difficult our relationships would be if we knew that our new father was once our own son. Or if we were aware that he was someone who did us great harm in another time and place. This knowledge would not help a person feel connected to their father so that they could build an appropriate relationship and ego structures to have a healthy, productive life.

Finally, remember that what I have shared with you is yours to experience. The lessons imparted in these pages are not to be taken on faith. Faith is a jumping-off point, but it should not be considered a destination. I do not consider myself a participant in a faith or belief system, but rather a knowledge and experience system. My telling you that a thing is so is not the same as your learning the truth of it. *Fire is hot and it will burn you* is a good piece of information, but until you have placed your hand over the flame, you will not truly know it.

Krishna taught Arjun much in Gita, and through him, teaches these lessons to us, but he never advocates that we ought to simply have faith. He never instructs us to believe something just because he said it was so. He emphasizes that we should learn these things deeply and truly for ourselves through our experiences and experiments. If you are open to the truths discussed in this book, they can be part of your life, and there's no need for me to try to convince you of any of it. Instead, I say to you: Don't believe. Just live and find out.

Extended About the Author

K RISHNA BHATTA, MD, FRCS IS an author, surgeon and an inventor, currently practicing as chief of urology at Northern Light Eastern Maine Medical Center in Bangor, Maine. Dr. Bhatta began his life in a small Indian village, attended Patna Medical College in India, continued his education in the UK, and then completed his research & medical training at Massachusetts General Hospital in Boston before settling down in Maine. His wife, Nayantara, is an OB/GYN and their two children are also physicians. Dr. Bhatta is former president of Maine Medical Association and Maine urology Society.

Dr. Bhatta is equal parts practical and spiritual, who developed fascination with spiritual studies early in his life. He speaks and writes prolifically on meditation and spiritual topics, and frequently travels across the globe to meditate at holy sites and speak with luminaries from various spiritual traditions. His lectures, writings, podcasts, songs, and video talks on Gita, Krishna, and other spiritual topics are based on his personal journey and experiences, as well as a lifetime of exploring spiritual texts, giving him a unique understanding and perspective.

Dr. Bhatta takes joy in sharing what he has learned and earnestly hopes to further the spiritual discoveries of generations to come.

Made in the USA
Las Vegas, NV
19 June 2021